the
FRAZZLED
FEMALE

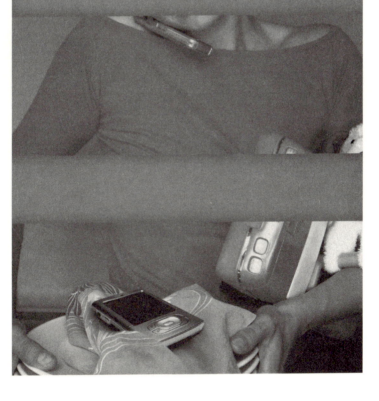

the
FRAZZLED
FEMALE

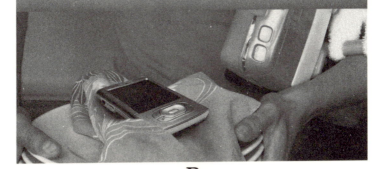

Finding God's Peace in Your Daily Chaos
CINDI WOOD

BROADMAN
& HOLMAN
PUBLISHERS
NASHVILLE, TENNESSEE

Ten-digit ISBN: 0-8054-4069-0
Thirteen-digit ISBN: 978-0-8054-4069-0

Published by Broadman & Holman Publishers
Nashville, Tennessee

Dewey Decimal Classification: 248.843
Subject Heading: STRESS (PSYCHOLOGY) \
MENTAL HEALTH \ WOMEN

Unless otherwise noted, all Scripture references are taken from the Holman Christian Standard Bible® © 1999, 2000, 2001, 2003 by Holman Bible Publishers. Other versions include: NIV, New International Version, copyright © 1973, 1978, 1984 by International Bible Society; CEV, the Contemporary English Version, © American Bible Society 1991, 1992; used by permission; and AMP, The Amplified Bible, Old Testament copyright © 1962, 1964 by Zondervan Publishing House, used by permission, and the New Testament © The Lockman Foundation 1954, 1958, 1987 used by permission.

1 2 3 4 5 6 7 8 9 10   10 09 08 07 06

Contents

Introducing . . .
The Frazzled Female

> **Frazzled Female**
> (fraz-eld fee-mal) n 1: a woman of the twenty-first century who is stressed, frayed, challenged, frenetic . . . and totally dependent on God to keep all the segments of her life together;
> 2: YOU?

I remember clearly when I first accepted the fact that I had joined the ranks of women who classified themselves as "frazzled." Actually they didn't call it that, but they wore the look, walked the walk, and talked the talk.

I saw no one sporting frazzled tees or wearing frazzled designer jeans, but yet most women I knew had the invisible insignia FRAZZLED embossed on their foreheads.

You *do* know what I mean, don't you?

Here's what *frazzled* looks like, sounds like, and walks like.

The Look

- A "wannabe" fresh radiant face that can't quite make it
- A not-so-put-together outfit that used to be in style
- Signs of wear and tear on a body that was at one time of life in pretty good shape

- Traces of twitching caused by an overloaded central nervous system

The Sound

- Less than positive words reflecting a "what-the-heck" attitude
- Strange noises caused by gastric juices jumping around in the stomach area
- A tone of voice that more often reflects misery, disgust, and "I've had all I can take" instead of joy

The Walk

- A heavy gait giving one the appearance of carrying an oversized dirty laundry bag as opposed to a light, springy step
- A body that doesn't move like it used to due to too many days of "I don't have time to exercise"
- Hunched shoulders from carrying too many burdens for too many people

Whether married or used to be married, single, with kids or without, working on the home front or out in the work world (or both), you may qualify for membership in the Frazzled Female Club!

The Frazzled Female Ministry is a ministry reaching out to all females who long for more peace and sanity in daily living. Women gathering for luncheons, seminars, or weekend retreats all share the same goal: seeking a life that's less stressful and more fulfilling every day, not just occasionally. It's my joy to share with women from all walks of life how to begin and then continue to live a victorious life—one that is not free from stress but one that is lived with the confidence, power, and peace that an intimate relationship with Jesus Christ offers!

One thing's for sure. Living life on the twenty-first century fast track is not easy. But girls, there's hope. *And hope's name is Jesus Christ!*

I'm excited for you to explore the pages of *The Frazzled Female* so you can learn how a relationship with Jesus can help you discover peace and joy, not to mention sanity. And this peace and joy will begin to affect the way you walk, the way you talk, and the way you look.

Read on, sister, and dare to imagine that a frazzled life can also be a joyful one and a more sane one than you've ever imagined. That's the promise and assurance that a life lived day in and day out with Jesus offers.

Victoriously frazzled,
Cindi Wood

PART ONE

Mary Chose the One Thing Needed, So Will I!

"But seek first the kingdom of God and His righteousness, and all these things will be provided for you."
MATTHEW 6:33

Do I sleep for five more minutes? What am I going to fix for supper tonight? Do I really need to stay for that meeting after work? So . . . do I exercise now or put it off until tomorrow?

Oh my, so many choices! Have you ever considered how many choices you make in any given day? Whether it's choosing your attitude or your clothing, those choices you make can critically impact your day (and the day of those around you)! The choices you make will determine how your day goes.

I remember the moment as a young mother that I chose to put my two-year-old son, Brandon, on a leash at the shopping mall. I ditched my pride along with my concern about what others might think of me strapping a leash to my son as if he were an animal.

And I can tell you, for me, securing that leash was a good choice, a sound choice, and a choice that brought freedom for me to enjoy being out with my little guy and not having to spend all that time racing around after him. (Besides, if I had not made that choice, we would have never left the house!)

Every day as a busy woman you make countless choices, choices that have to do with everything from household duties to self-improvement to professional development. So it's truly important that you consider your options carefully.

No matter how many choices I make during any given day, I have discovered that the most important one for me and the one that has the greatest impact on how my day goes is to *choose* to spend time with Jesus at the beginning of my day.

Now most of the time that means getting up earlier than I would if I just hopped out of bed and jumped on my to-do list. But I've realized that my day is not half as good (or productive) if I don't have that quiet time with Jesus. Without choosing to be with him first, before I tackle anything else, I'm pretty agitated, strung out, and soon run out of energy. I have just learned that about me! So the most important choice I make every day, the choice that determines the flow of the rest of my day, is to be with Jesus right when I wake up and before I do anything else.

Now, before you think I'm endowed with some sort of special equipment that enables me to tune into Jesus when my eyes pop open in the morning, let me rush to tell you that I haven't always been this way. Choosing him first has not always been my practice. Making this choice is a process, just like choosing to exercise or eat right or invest some money into a savings account. You choose to spend time with him one day at a time until that choice becomes your lifestyle.

One of the things I've done that has helped transition my daily choice into a lifestyle change was to create a rendezvous place for my quiet time with God. There's a special place each morning where I sit with him, reading some Scripture and talking to him. "My spot" is at my kitchen bar. Before I go to bed, I create an inviting place to spend time with him the following morning. Sometimes I place a candle or a small lamp close by, as well as my Bible and notepad to record my thoughts. When I walk into my kitchen the following morning, I just ease into enjoying this time with Jesus. Other women have shared with me that they enjoy their devotional time in a corner of a guest bedroom, or a deck in warm weather, or even a section of a big closet.

There's nothing magical about having a special location. It's just a comfortable spot that you set aside for your time with him.

You see, the practice of creating a warm and inviting place to meet Jesus is to help you move forward into choosing a lifestyle that gets you rollin' with him as soon as your eyes open! And when you make it a practice to spend time with him each morning, you will find that gradually your days begin to be filled with more peace and joy and less frustration and irritation.

You'll also learn other strategies throughout this book that will help you connect with God throughout your day whether you're in heavy traffic or stuck in a line at the grocery store.

The foundation that holds the content of this book is the encounter between Jesus, Mary, and Martha as found in Luke 10 of the New Testament. We'll explore it a little more deeply later, but for now let's just say that in this passage Mary made the choice of being with Jesus while Martha, her sister, busied herself with the day's tasks.

The Scriptures allow us to step into one of Mary's quiet encounters with him. And this quiet time was at a very unlikely time; it was a quiet encounter during the very moments that her sister Martha was "[overly occupied and too busy] . . . distracted with much serving" (Luke 10:40 AMP).

In this passage Jesus uses the choice Martha made to teach us and invite us into a vibrant, living, and powerful relationship with him—a relationship that greatly impacts every moment of your every day, if you choose to enter into it!

Chapter One

He Loves Me!

"I will be the same until your old age, and I will bear you up
when you turn gray. I have made you, and I will carry you;
I will bear and save you."

ISAIAH 46:4

The movie was ending. Although Anna enjoyed the film, watching the sappy love story on TV made her feel she was missing out on something in life. Ed and Sally were caught up in a passionate romance. They had no children, jobs that left them with plenty of time to be together, and plenty of energy to take care of each other's needs. They spent hours talking and enjoying each other's company. Every part of their lives was absolutely wonderful because of the intimacy of their love!

I'll never experience that kind of love, was the thought that played over and over in Anna's mind.

We perceive love in all sorts of ways. Whether we connect love with someone helping us around the house, sending flowers, complimenting the way we dress, or writing a mushy note, women crave LOVE!

Depending on our age, circumstances, and immediate needs, our definition of *love* varies. For instance, to my ninety-seven-year-old grandmother, love is sitting and talking eyeball to eyeball with her. My sixteen-year-old niece, Kyra, experiences love when I spend the day shopping with her, while my daughter-in-law Bonnie loves it when we take a hike up the mountain together. Whatever form love takes, when we experience it, it meets our basic needs for security and significance.

In Dr. Gary Chapman's book *The Five Love Languages,* he addresses the significance of feeling loved. "I am significant. Life has meaning. There is a higher purpose. I want to believe it, but I may not feel significant until someone expresses love to me. Without love, I may spend a lifetime in search of significance, self-worth, and security. When I experience love, it impacts all of those needs positively. I am now freed to develop my potential."[1]

Now let me tell you about love, about *true* love. The true love story of every believer is the journey of her heart. The one who loves you the most calls out to your heart every moment. Jesus longs for you to spend time in his presence, listening to his voice. In the middle of your daily stresses, he wants to have a relationship with you. He wants you to step back from all the good things you are doing to experience the *best* thing, an intimate relationship with him! He wants to say about you what he said about Mary, "But one thing is necessary. Mary has made the right choice, and it will not be taken away from her" (Luke 10:42).

Many women work hard doing so many good things for so many people that they bypass the one thing in life that's most important, and that's an intimate love relationship with Jesus. God wants us to minister to and meet the needs of others; however, our time with him is more important to him than anything we can do for him. Out of this love relationship, a lifestyle of doing things for others will naturally flow.

If you have already accepted Jesus Christ as your personal Lord and Savior, then he is longing for you to experience a deep and satisfying love relationship with him on a daily basis. He wants to give your life deeper meaning, filling each area of your life with his peace and his joy. And he wants to do this right in the middle of your daily stress!

Now if you haven't invited Jesus to live in your heart but you are yearning to experience an out-of-this-world love relationship, then the good news for you is the same good news that countless women have experienced as they have chosen to invite Jesus Christ to be the Lord of their lives. I invite you to turn to "How to Become a Christian" on page 120, to learn how to begin your personal relationship with Jesus Christ.

≈ Have you invited Jesus Christ to live in your heart?

≈ Do you desire a deeper relationship with him?

Chapter Two

The Journey of Intimacy

"But Martha was distracted by her many tasks, and she came up and asked, 'Lord, don't You care that my sister has left me to serve alone? So tell her to give me a hand.'"
LUKE 10:40

Micki had heard about Mary and Martha for as long as she could remember. Pastors, teachers, and Christian speakers all pointed to Mary as the ultimate example of the devoted follower of God. Micki also recalled the picture her fourth-grade Sunday school teacher painted of Martha being too busy even to notice Jesus while Mary did nothing but sit and listen as he talked. Even as a child, Micki remembered thinking, *How could anybody just sit and listen when there were so many things to do?* As an adult, she realized her feelings were much the same.

We live in a world constantly screaming to get our attention! Women tell me they don't have time to exercise and eat right. No time to clean their houses or spend quality time with their family and friends, and certainly no time even to consider doing something special for themselves.

How then can we possibly think it's realistic to enter into a personal and growing relationship with Jesus Christ? *That takes time!*

To have the proper view of Mary, we must understand the nature of "sitting at his feet." For me it's being preoccupied with God. Each day I pull back from all other responsibilities and sit quietly with him. Most of the time this is early in the morning when I begin my day. I read my Bible, sing softly to him, talk to him about what's in store for me that day, and pray for my needs and the needs of others.

Now there's another way I "sit at his feet." I call it *emotionally and mentally sitting at the feet of Jesus*. It's simply thinking about him throughout my day. I ask him to go to the bank with me, help me as I get my groceries, be my companion as I drive across town, and give me the words I need before I make a telephone call. I invite him to become involved in every detail of my life.

To be honest with you, some days I'm better at this than others. Some days I'm like Mary, longing to be with Jesus and being aware of him throughout the entire day. And then there are those other days, the days I'm like Martha—inviting him in but immediately going about my daily duties, neglecting his presence and never asking for his help, or forgetting that I *did* ask him for his help.

Let's look at this well-known passage from Luke 10. Perhaps you can identify with one (or both) of these sisters as you think about your typical day.

> Now while they were on their way, it occurred that Jesus entered a certain village, and a woman named Martha received and welcomed Him into her house. And she had a sister named Mary, who seated herself at the Lord's feet and was listening to His teaching. But Martha [overly occupied and too busy] was distracted with much serving; and she came up to Him and said, Lord, is it nothing to You that my sister has left me to serve alone? Tell her then to help me [to lend a hand and do her part along with me]! But the Lord replied to her by

saying, Martha, Martha, you are anxious and troubled about many things; there is need of only one or but a few things. Mary has chosen the good portion [that which is to her advantage], which shall not be taken away from her. (Luke 10:38–42 AMP)

On the days I'm like Martha, as described in this passage, I welcome Jesus into my day when I first get up in the morning, but then I become *overly occupied and too busy* with everything I have to do, forgetting to acknowledge his presence and forgetting to ask him for his help.

I'm most like Mary when I spend time with him first thing in the morning and then continue to think about him throughout the day as I run though my never ending to-do list, inviting him to be a part of each and every thing that occupies my mind, my energy, and my time!

You see, your heavenly Father longs for you to think about him as you go about your daily activities. Can you believe it? Honestly, it amazes me when I really think about that fact. It's just so hard to believe that Jesus would want to spend time with *me*, in all of the little "nothing kinds of things" that fill most of my days. Truth is, he wants to be part of every detail of my life and yours too, whether you're planning dinner or cleaning your desk at the office or scrubbing your messy bathroom.

In desiring to spend time with you, your heavenly Father is longing to fill your life with wonderful blessings.

In the Amplified version of the Bible, we capture the full meaning behind the original Greek text. In verse 42 Jesus responds to Martha, "Mary has chosen the good portion [that which is to her advantage], which shall not be taken away from her."

An *advantage* is a favorable circumstance, a benefit. As we grow in intimacy with our Lord, we will notice many benefits.

Here are some benefits that women share with me that they have experienced as they grow closer to God:

"I am much calmer than usual."

"I'm laughing more and enjoying life."

"Things don't get to me like they used to."

"My children and I are getting along better."

"I'm not as short-tempered as I used to be."

"My life seems to have more meaning."

"The more time I spend with Jesus, the more
I grow to love him."

Of all the benefits mentioned, the last one seems to sum up this love relationship! I spend time with Jesus because I love him. The more my love grows, the more I long to spend time with him.

Then out of this love relationship, I experience many benefits, and so do the people around me!

My friend, if you're longing for more joy, peace, and—yes—excitement in your life, then I offer you the reality that a growing relationship with Jesus will help you discover all of these qualities. If you're longing to have a close friend and to have a reason for living, then you can ask your heavenly Father to help you grow that relationship with him. If you ask him, he will give you the desire to become more aware of him throughout your day as he begins to fill your life with his peace in the midst of your frazzledness.

- What advantages do you want in your life?

- Are you willing to commit to a quiet time with Jesus on a daily basis?

Chapter Three

Hearing When God Speaks

"He said to them, 'Come away by yourselves to a remote
place and rest a while.'"
MARK 6:31

One of the exciting benefits I notice as I continue to grow
my love relationship with Jesus is the inner peace he gives
to me. Going to that quiet place enables me to rest my mind
and tone down my emotions.

It's an ongoing and gradual process. I still remember
the excitement I felt as a small child, as I inched upward on
the measuring stick that my mom kept tucked away beside
the washer.

It's the same principle for measuring your "growth" with
the Lord. A wonderful love relationship doesn't just happen
overnight, and the beauty of the process is the joy that you feel
as you grow closer and closer to him.

Unlike any other love relationship you experience, this
quest for intimacy is divinely propelled. God loves for you to
desire to grow close to him, and he longs to delight your heart
with his love!

If you've thought of *intimacy with God* as a goal that could
never be reached, I hope you'll reconsider. *Intimate* means

"deep and personal." So an intimate relationship with Jesus Christ is one that is deep and personal. And it's not like you ever totally arrive. You just keep growing deeper and more personal with him, and the whole process of growing in your intimacy with him can be a beautifully satisfying journey.

In our relationship with Jesus, intimacy becomes a goal that is ever before us and one that we can celebrate each step of the way.

In the period of the Old Testament, God sometimes spoke audibly. Scripture records the experience of Samuel, a young boy who had been taken to the tabernacle to be raised by the priest Eli. Samuel had not yet begun an intimate relationship with God, and he had never heard his voice. After hearing him speak three times, Samuel finally recognized the voice to be the voice of God.

> The boy Samuel served the LORD in Eli's presence. In those days the word of the LORD was rare and prophetic visions were not widespread.
>
> One day Eli, whose eyesight was failing, was lying in his room. Before the lamp of God had gone out, Samuel was lying down in the tabernacle of the LORD where the ark of God was located.
>
> Then the LORD called Samuel, and he answered, "Here I am." He ran to Eli and said, "Here I am; you called me."
>
> "I didn't call," Eli replied. "Go and lie down." So he went and lay down.
>
> Once again the LORD called, "Samuel!"
>
> Samuel got up, went to Eli, and said, "Here I am; you called me."
>
> "I didn't call, my son," he replied. "Go and lie down."
>
> Now Samuel had not yet experienced the LORD, because the word of the LORD had not yet been revealed to him. Once again, for the third time, the

LORD called Samuel. He got up, went to Eli, and said, "Here I am; you called me."

Then Eli understood that the LORD was calling the boy. He told Samuel, "Go and lie down. If He calls you, say, 'Speak, LORD, for Your servant is listening.'" So Samuel went and lay down in his place.

The LORD came, stood there, and called as before, "Samuel, Samuel!"

Samuel responded, "Speak, for Your servant is listening." (1 Sam. 3:1–10)

Samuel thought it was the priest Eli speaking to him. He was quick to respond when he heard his name called but did not recognize the voice of the Lord. Three times God called out to him. Each time Samuel rushed to the elder priest and answered, "Here I am." After the third time, Eli perceived that it was the Lord calling the boy.

As I think about my growing relationship with God, I'm aware that he speaks to me in many ways. I often sense him speaking to me as I read my Bible. Sometimes I'm particularly close to him and sense his voice when I'm surrounded by nature. There are times a friend calls me and I'm sure that what she says is straight from God. And at other times he sings straight to my heart through beautiful music.

When I'm thinking about God or at least aware of his presence, it's easier for me to "hear" him. If my mind becomes preoccupied with all I have to do, or if some negative thought keeps creeping in, it's harder for me to discern his voice.

It's natural to be preoccupied with life. Great demands are placed upon you in all the roles you play. You may be much like Samuel, simply preoccupied with your duties and not recognizing God's voice.

But God keeps calling your name. He is so persistent with his love! He wants to enter into your busy schedule and minister to you and soothe you with his peace and his joy. Through spending time with him and thinking about him throughout your day, you *will* begin to recognize his voice. And recognizing his voice means experiencing him. Experiencing God means being aware of his presence, his love, his joy, and his peace.

Someone may say something to you in conversation, and you know it is a word from God. Sometimes you may become acutely aware of beauty in nature and hear God speaking. You may recall a Scripture passage during the day that speaks to a certain need, issue, or circumstance. These are all examples of God speaking to you!

The fourth time the Lord spoke to Samuel, the boy responded, "Speak, for Your servant is listening" (1 Sam. 3:10). This passage reveals the consistency of God! He's unchanging in his love for us. Just as he continued to call Samuel, he continues to speak to us and pursue us wherever we are and whatever we are doing.

When I think about little Samuel, I can just imagine that he was excited when he finally realized it was God who was calling him. Excitement and joy are always present when you "hook up" with God. When you desire to know God and begin to seek him with all your heart, you'll begin to experience him in ways you never thought possible.

I always want the response of my heart to be, "Speak to me, Father. I'm listening!"

- ☞ Have you ever felt like God was speaking to you?

- ☞ Do you think you could "hear" him more if you spent more time quietly in his presence?

Chapter Four

My Heart's Longing

"The LORD is near the brokenhearted;
He saves those crushed in spirit."
PSALM 34:18

Women are programmed with intense emotions and the capacity to yearn for life's best for themselves, their families, and their friends. God has equipped us with desires so deep that when those desires go unmet we often experience pain—physical, emotional, and mental!

Women in Frazzled Female sessions have told me that the longings they experience are often so intense that they consume their every thought.

My friend Kaye and I were friends long before she married in her forties. I remember the deeply emotional conversations we had about the longing of her heart to be married and to be a mom. Kaye had a relationship with Jesus Christ, and she gave this burden to him, but on many days she still felt unfulfilled.

I know other Christian women who, because of preoccupation with the intense longings of their heart, often experience sleepless nights, lack of energy, and extreme weariness.

If you, like me, and like scores of other women have ever experienced those unfulfilled longings, then let me assure you, *God knows the longing of your heart!* And furthermore he cares all about your deep desires and longs to fulfill your deepest needs.

I have listened as many women have poured out their heartaches to our loving God. The longings are as varied as the women themselves. While some women long for children, others long for Christian husbands. Some yearn to serve God in ministry, and others are preoccupied with desires for their children. Whatever the deep desire of your life at this time, be assured that God knows, he understands, and he truly longs to be the answer to your need.

In the last chapter we read about little Samuel. Before his birth his mother Hannah experienced the heart-wrenching turbulence of a longing unfulfilled. In ancient Hebrew society for a wife to have no children was a terrible trial. She not only felt lonely and unfulfilled as a woman, but she also carried the burden of feeling she had displeased God. Since children were viewed as gifts from God, Hannah experienced a deep sense of guilt as well as the reproach of others.

The following Scripture takes place upon her visit to the temple where she was pouring out the longing of her heart to God. Eli the priest was there, observing her display of intense emotions.

> Deeply hurt, Hannah prayed to the LORD and wept with many tears. Making a vow, she pleaded, "LORD of Hosts, if You will take notice of Your servant's affliction, remember and not forget me, and give Your servant a son, I will give him to the LORD all the days of his life, and his hair will never be cut."

> While she was praying in the LORD's presence, Eli watched her lips. Hannah was speaking to herself, and although her lips were moving, her voice

could not be heard. Eli thought she was drunk and scolded her, "How long are you going to be drunk? Get rid of your wine!"

"No, my lord," Hannah replied. "I am a woman with a broken heart. I haven't had any wine or beer; I've been pouring out my heart before the LORD. Don't think of me as a wicked woman; I've been praying from the depth of my anguish and resentment." (1 Sam. 1:10–16)

This passage almost makes me laugh. While I identify with the way Hannah poured her deep longing to the Lord, it amuses me that Eli thought she was drunk! I wonder if she knew he was looking. I tend to be quite theatrical when I'm alone with the Lord, laying my deepest needs before him, and it makes me sheepishly smile to think of someone looking in on those private and personal moments!

God wants you to lay it all out before him. He wants you to turn your soul inside out to him; and whatever you are experiencing on the inside, he wants you to bring every bit of it to him—anger, frustration, helplessness, fatigue, whatever.

First Samuel 1:10 in the NIV reads, "In bitterness of soul Hannah wept much and prayed to the LORD." Now if you identify with Hannah in the intensity of her longing, then you most likely identify with her bitterness. Hannah may have felt that she had reason to feel bitter about life and even about God. Circumstances in life can lead us to bitterness and may even cause us to question God's love for us.

God wants us to bring such thoughts to him. He longs for us to bring our sorrow, our bitterness, our heartbreak to him so he can comfort us and ultimately give us the desires of our hearts.

Yes, Hannah did exactly what God wants us to do. Instead of allowing her distress to get the best of her, she took her sorrow to the Lord. Prayer is the only way to gain strength to overcome both your emotions and your circumstances.

Dear friend, when I continue to run to him with my burden, my focus gradually shifts from my burden to my God. As I spend more time talking to him about my deep desires, I begin to realize that he is reaching into my soul and is saturating my inner being with a desire for him. Sticking with God when my prayers seem unanswered is only possible with the Lord's help.

Romans 8:26–27 tells us, "In the same way the Spirit also joins to help in our weakness, because we do not know what to pray for as we should, but the Spirit Himself intercedes for us with unspoken groanings. And He who searches the hearts knows the Spirit's mind-set, because He intercedes for the saints according to the will of God."

Persistent praying is the realization, based on faith, that he sees my need and longs to help me. This kind of praying takes me deeper into intimacy with the Almighty Father. If we allow him, God uses our longing as a divine tool to bring us deeper into a relationship with him.

As you turn your desires over to God, you invite him to bless you by giving you his answer to your particular need. If God denies your request, he has something better planned for your life. I have come to the place in my life of choosing to give my yearnings to the Lord, followed with the prayer, "But Father, if you have something better in mind, cancel my request." That kind of prayer can only come from an intimate relationship based in faith and the knowledge that God's will for my life is always best!

God always answers prayers. "In my distress I called to the Lord, and He answered me" (Ps. 120:1). We must realize that his answer may not be in our way or in our timing, but he always answers!

I pray that you are beginning to birth a willing spirit, offering him the longing of your heart so that he may bring you closer into his love and meet your deepest need. In asking him to give you what he knows is best for your life, you are placing your trust in the one who has every need of your heart covered. In turning to him, you can be absolutely confident that what he has in mind for you is better than anything you could ever imagine. And remember, total faith and reliance on him will not happen overnight but will gradually grow as you spend time with him, pouring out your heart and trusting him to give you his best!

- ☞ Do you have an unfilled need in your life?

- ☞ Can you trust God to meet this deep longing of your heart?

Chapter Five

Something More

*"You will seek Me and find Me when you search
for Me with all your heart."*
JEREMIAH 29:13

Patti had been a Christian for many years. She loved the
Lord and enjoyed being involved in church. That's why it
surprised her to realize she was becoming dissatisfied with life.
It wasn't anything she could put her finger on; she just didn't
feel like spending time with God the way she used to, and she
wasn't enjoying the time she did spend with him. She was busy
doing good things, God's things. All of her free time was spent
doing things that revolved around her love for the Lord. She
wondered what was happening in her walk with God. Why did
she feel so blah?

There may be many times during your Christian walk
when "life with God" seems less than exciting. And that experience seems to become painfully obvious if you have ever once
experienced a vibrant relationship with Jesus Christ. It's easy to
get discouraged when you don't feel that excitement and joy.

Consider the following reasons that may contribute to the
loss of zeal in your relationship with him:

- Unconfessed sin
- Problems with people

BOONE COUNTY

4482993

- Difficulty focusing on God
- Being preoccupied with other things
- Not taking time to sit still in his presence
- God creating the dissatisfaction

I am learning that when I go through those times of spiritual dissatisfaction to cry out with the words of the psalmist, "Search me, God, and know my heart; test me and know my concerns. See if there is any offensive way in me; lead me in the everlasting way" (Ps. 139:23–24).

When I pray this prayer, he gives me a sense of what's wrong. It may be that I am caught up in concerns of my own, distracting my focus, or I may just be so busy that I'm not slowing down enough to talk quietly with him.

I've also discovered that willful and/or unconfessed sin in my heart will create a barrier between God and me. These may be obvious sins that I'm aware of and just refusing to turn my heart to him in repentance, or they may be sins that I'm unconsciously harboring in my thought life. That's why praying the prayer of Psalm 139 brings unconscious sins to light. As I pray that prayer, God either reveals an area of sin in my life so that I can confess it or gives me peace that sin is not the reason for the distance I am experiencing.

In the book of Colossians, Paul writes to struggling Christians. He encourages them to be strengthened and comforted, having their roots firmly planted in Jesus and overflowing with thanksgiving. "Therefore as you have received Christ Jesus the Lord, walk in Him, rooted and built up in Him and established in the faith, just as you were taught, and overflowing with thankfulness" (Col. 2:6–7).

You need plenty of faith to be joyful when you don't feel the joy. Life on earth is like that. Sometimes you just don't feel happy. But Paul encourages us to remember what we were taught and to continue to overflow with thanksgiving.

When I experience a void in my spiritual life, it usually leads me to want more of God, to thirst after him. In one of the greatest invitations ever offered, Jesus stood up in the middle of the crowds in Jerusalem and said, "If anyone is thirsty, he should come to Me and drink!" (John 7:37).

Thinking about it, the reason I first came to Jesus was because of my thirst for him and my longing to experience his love and salvation. And the longer I live with him, the more I desire to grow closer and closer to him! So when I feel a distance in our relationship, I'm driven to keep searching and praying until I figure out why the distance is there.

The apostle Paul viewed intimacy with Christ as the supreme goal in his life. His goal for all believers, as recorded in Colossians 2:2, is that they "be encouraged and joined together in love, so that they may have all the riches of assured understanding, and have the knowledge of God's mystery—Christ."

Speaking of that "distance" thing, when we get too busy with too many things, even good things, our focus moves from the Lord to whatever we are doing. It's also easy for us to become distracted because of our emotions, or people, or the feeling that we just don't have time.

You need to encourage you to push through those times when you are less than excited about your love relationship with Jesus. Just talk to him about it. Tell him about your dissatisfaction in your relationship and ask him to create a desire in you that will bring you closer to him.

I can assure you, based on the authority of God's Word, that he will never turn his back on a heart that seeks him. Feeling distant from God is not geographical. It's personal! If Jesus Christ lives in your heart, then you are *always* in his presence. There may be times when you do not feel this closeness, but he's there and he's not going anywhere. According to Hebrews 13:5 his promise to us is, "I will never leave you or forsake you."

As we move into the next section, we'll be exploring how a positive attitude can help you in deepening your relationship with Jesus. He longs for you to enjoy his presence, and he's all about equipping you with everything you need to experience life at its fullest!

- ☞ Do you ever feel distant from God?

- ☞ Are you willing to seek him and allow him to reveal to you why you feel distant?

PART TWO

A Less Than Positive Attitude

"Pleasant words are a honeycomb: sweet to the taste
and health to the body."
PROVERBS 16:24

A positive attitude does not take care of all your problems,
but it sure will help you have at least a little bit of your
sanity left by the end of the day!

Some months ago I was headed home after a three-day
Frazzled Female event. Feeling rather exhausted, I was looking forward to sleeping during the hour-and-a-half flight. As
soon as I snuggled up in my little cubby next to the window,
I heard the piercing cry of a baby somewhere behind me.
"Oh no!" I sighed as my thoughts of slumber quickly drowned
in the chaos that was happening several rows back.

If that poor mother was feeling stressed out and exasperated, it wasn't half as much as the passengers in rows one
through twenty! The screaming continued through the
instructions on safety belts, oxygen masks, flotation devices,
and emergency exiting (which I was strongly considering).

Just when I had convinced myself that I could and *I would* stand anything for an hour and a half, the captain's voice came over the speaker, "Ladies and gentlemen, I'm sorry to inform you that due to weather conditions we are having to delay our flight. Since we are next in line for takeoff, we'll just sit right here until we're cleared to go. I apologize for this inconvenience. Try to relax and enjoy yourselves during the wait."

And I did try to relax as Baby X surpassed any previous attempts I had heard at being number one in the division of Loud-Screaming-With-No-Breathing category.

I knew very well this was a test! God was checking me out to see if I really believed everything I had spoken just hours ago about *choosing* a positive attitude in the midst of trying and stressful circumstances. Just as I was considering whether I would pass the positive test, I looked across the aisle and noticed the pain-plastered look on the face of the woman seated there. She was clenching her teeth and holding her head. I touched her on the arm as I said, "Do you have grown children?" A mere nod told me that she did, to which I exclaimed, "Aren't you glad!"

That halfhearted attempt to make a little stab at humor, when I felt anything but joyful, paid off. My new support sister and I spent time talking, laughing, and swapping tales of crying babies and depleted moms.

When you choose a positive attitude, you're choosing an attitude with muscle! A positive attitude strengthens you and equips you with hope and endurance to deal with whatever the circumstance may be.

And you know, that ol' plane did finally take off forty-five minutes later; and approximately one hour and a half after that, we landed, screaming baby and all, safely at home. And home never seemed sweeter (or quieter).

Chapter Six

A Positive Beginning

"Rejoice always! Pray constantly. Give thanks in everything, for this is God's will for you in Christ Jesus."
1 THESSALONIANS 5:16–18

Sometimes it takes sheer determination to choose to be positive. Being positive in the words we speak, the facial expressions we make, and the thoughts we think are opportunities of choice throughout any day. When I have a recurring negative thought—you know, one that just won't go away—I often choose to take a twenty-four-hour fast on negative thinking! Here's how it works: when a negative thought keeps interrupting what I am supposed to be thinking about, I just ZAP it, and I keep zapping it for the entire day. Now according to the laws of zapping, when you zap a thought, you have to put another thought in its place, or it won't stay zapped!

Here's how it works. Let's say you walk into the kitchen early in the morning to find a mess left by your daughter and her friends the night before. Instead of allowing your angry feelings to take over and ruin your morning, you immediately toss—*no throw*—the negative feeling out of your mind, determining to focus on a positive one. For me, the best positive thoughts are Scriptures. For this situation, how about: "Be glad in the LORD, you righteous ones, and praise His holy name" (Ps. 97:12).

You have to train yourself to apply this approach, as well as keep your arsenal of Scriptures close by. Believe me, thinking positively doesn't come naturally. Being upset and thinking negatively does! But when you respond to the situation, whatever it might be, in this way, then you're better equipped to address the situation later, like when your daughter gets up! Because you have made the choice to react positively instead of negatively, you are better equipped to deal with the problem rationally.

With this approach also, I know I can deal with some issues tomorrow if I still need to. And often I find that "tomorrow" takes care of the problem, and I don't even have to revisit it. Choosing to think positively fuels my energy, keeps me focused, and saves time!

One of my positive heroes in the Old Testament is Abraham. When God told Abraham to set out for a new land, Abraham chose to listen. He also chose to be positive about God's direction for his life. Abraham's obedience in his attitude and in his behavior caused him to be uprooted from his familiar way of life yet led him to discover God's greatness. He chose to trust even when God's promises seemed impossible to believe. Abraham sometimes strayed from the path by trying to work things out his way, but he continued to listen and be obedient as God called for his trust.

> The LORD said to Abram:
> Go out from your land,
>   your relatives,
>   and your father's house
>   to the land that I will show you.
> I will make you into a great nation,
> I will bless you,
> I will make your name great,
>   and you will be a blessing.

> I will bless those who bless you,
> I will curse those who treat you with contempt,
>   and all the peoples on earth
>   will be blessed through you.

So Abram went, as the LORD had told him, and
Lot went with him. Abram was 75 years old when he
left Haran. He took his wife Sarai, his nephew Lot,
all the possessions they had accumulated, and the
people he had acquired in Haran, and they set out
for the land of Canaan. (Gen. 12:1–5)

God called Abraham to leave his home and family and go
to a foreign country. I'm sure Abraham must have experienced
some intense emotions. Perhaps he was not really pleased that
God had asked him to do such an exciting thing. Maybe he
even doubted about what he thought God had said. He could
have been afraid about what people might think of him, doing
something so seemingly crazy. But nonetheless, even though
he didn't understand God's plan, he chose to trust him.

Anytime you move in obedience to God's call, it's a positive choice. Anytime you listen to God and obey his words,
you are moving in a positive direction. Sometimes God will
ask you to step out of your comfort zone and do something
that you are not naturally inclined to do. But if you follow
in obedience, any discomfort you experience will eventually
lead you to God's blessings.

As Abraham continued in his journey of obedience,
one small positive step at a time, the Lord continued to reveal
himself and his plan. Abraham, in turn, worshipped God. As
you grow in your walk with the Lord and gradually develop a
lifestyle of listening to him and obeying him, remember to worship him along the way. Worship is an integral part of developing a positive lifestyle. You can rejoice that your heavenly Father
is leading you and that you are following him in obedience.

Being positive involves more than what we think about.
For the Christian a positive attitude encompasses our whole

being. We become positive by listening to God, obediently following his directions, continually worshipping him, and seeking his presence.

☞ Generally speaking, would you be described as a positive person?

☞ In what area of your life do you tend to be the most negative?

Chapter Seven

You Become What You Think

"Lord, I turn my hope to You."
PSALM 25:1

Maybe you are beginning to identify areas in your life where you could grow a more positive attitude by listening to God a little more closely. And just maybe, he's impressing you about some specific circumstances where a positive attitude would be helpful.

When my sons were teenagers, I knew God was telling me to be a more positive mother. He was telling me to *look*, *speak*, and *act* in more positive ways. I soon discovered that being positive did not come naturally but being negative did! As I shared with you earlier, I realized that it was no easy thing to get rid of negative thinking. I frequently had to trash the negative thoughts. And I can tell you, this created plenty of room to store the positive ones. And if I didn't hurry and put the positive ones in, the negative ones would rush back in to fill the space! Your mind cannot hold a void. *Something* has to be in there! After various attempts with little success, I learned the best way to stop that negative flow was by plugging it with Scripture.

When you spend time meditating on the Word of God, you are taking hold of his supernatural power! There's not a self-help book anywhere that can equip you with the divine, supernatural power of God. That's why I choose to speak Scripture often throughout the day. The benefits I gain are totally indescribable. (The people around me greatly benefit too!)

"Finally brothers, whatever is true, whatever is honorable, whatever is just, whatever is pure, whatever is lovely, whatever is commendable—if there is any moral excellence and if there is any praise—dwell on these things" (Phil. 4:8).

Reflecting on this *powerful and supernaturally propelled* verse from Philippians helped me a lot, and I believe it will help guide you toward a positive lifestyle! If you begin to think about what you're thinking about and determine to place a positive thought in your mind when the negative one jumps up, then you're making progress.

For instance, if you dwell on your messy house, are you following the guidelines of this Scripture? No! If however, you think about how much you love your family who made that mess, you're on track!

Come on, friend, trash the negative thought that you *can't* be positive, and join with me as we tackle a more positive lifestyle together. It's an ongoing process, and on some days it's easier than on others, but the benefits of choosing to at least *try* to be positive greatly pay off.

Truth is, your positive or your negative lifestyle will indeed affect every function of your body. If you dwell on negative things, you will spout negative words and have negative facial expressions and body gestures. Being negative keeps you unproductive and focusing on self. When you think negatively, you simply do not accomplish as much in a day as you do when you think positively.

Dr. Charles Stanley writes about sowing to the flesh (catering to your negative thoughts) and sowing to the Spirit (choosing to think positively).

Every morning when you and I awaken, we begin sowing. In our minds, we sow thoughts—positive or negative, good or evil. In our actions, our attitudes, our habits all day long, we sow either to the flesh or to the Spirit. The things you sow in the Spirit are life producing and have the potential for eternal reward. The very nature of the Holy Spirit is life, and the things you sow to the Spirit produce a zest for living. They have an ability to produce, multiply, and flourish into an abundant harvest. The more you sow to the Spirit, the greater the harvest of things that result in your ability to achieve the goals that God has helped you set.[2]

Sowing to the Spirit, being positive will help you accomplish all that God wants you to accomplish!

Are you ready to take on a more positive lifestyle? Becoming the positive person God wants you to be begins with examining your negative thinking. Here's a sampling of negative thoughts I've collected from "wannabe" positive thinkers:

I can't stand going home to a messy house after I work hard all day at the office.

Thinking about cooking tonight makes me sick.

If only my husband would help out with the kids.

Washing, cleaning, cooking, running . . . I never get any thanks.

This job stinks. I wish I could do something I like.

Life's just one chore after another.

There's never enough time for me.

If she weren't such a busybody, she'd get more done.

Could you add a few (or ten or twenty) thoughts, yourself? It's easy to think negatively. It's also the natural thing to do. Truth is, all of these negative thoughts may even be reality for you. You may feel that many situations in your life have *created* your bad attitude. A lot of people feel that way. But take a look at what Paul (who was in prison at the time of this writing) says in divinely breathed Scripture. "Rejoice in the Lord always. I will say it again: Rejoice!" (Phil. 4:4).

So you see my friend, according to Scripture, it's not a suggestion but a command to rejoice in the midst of all things. It won't happen overnight, but with determination you will gradually become more positive. At the end of the day, if you've had more positive thoughts than negative ones, then you're making progress! And with that movement of obedience comes God's grace, his blessing, and a positive attitude!

- ☞ Does negative thinking keep you from accomplishing your goals?

- ☞ Can you identify some negative thoughts that could be replaced by positive ones?

Chapter Eight

The Power of God

"For in Him we live and move and exist."
ACTS 17:28

All week Debbie had been looking forward to sleeping in on Saturday. Every day she had gotten up at her usual abnormally early time just to get things done. Her week was filled with putting out fires—everybody else's. People were always wanting her to do something but were never satisfied with anything she did. Every time she made a little progress with her work, she had to add another item to her to-do list.

Early in the week Debbie promised God she would really try to have a more positive attitude. She told him she wanted to spend more time with him to soak in his goodness and joy. However, she had an aging parent who took much of her time and a family that didn't help with housework. By the end of the week she was exhausted and grumpy. The only thing she looked forward to was sleeping late on Saturday morning.

On Friday night, Erin, Debbie's friend, called telling her that her husband, Jeff, had to report to work at seven the following morning. Erin was sick and wondered if Debbie could keep two-year-old Carly on Saturday. Jeff could drop her off on his way to work.

It is so easy for those good intentions for a positive attitude to be annihilated when a week soars high on the stress scale! I don't know about you, but if I were Debbie at the end of that particular week, I would be so tempted to pretend the phone lines were blotched up and I couldn't hear a thing that Erin said!

Oh my! Life can be so frustrating! It's such a challenge to react positively when stressors are continually thrown your way. I have found that many times we women can handle the big things in life that produce stress. Maybe it's because we've planned in advance for them and realize they are coming. However, the accumulation of common daily hassles often sneaks up on us and robs our joy and positive attitude.

What's a woman to do? Well, you can *try* to do better, but trying in your own strength results in major frustration! Instead of relying on my own positive dealing ability, I'm getting better at recognizing God's power in my life! He can put that positive attitude back where it belongs and keep me from getting helplessly frustrated when the little (and big) things pile up.

We believers forget that it is the power of Jesus Christ living within us that enables us to become more Christlike in having a positive attitude! Paul talks about it in Ephesians:

> I pray that the God of our Lord Jesus Christ,
> the glorious Father, would give you a spirit of wisdom and revelation in the knowledge of Him.
> I pray that the eyes of your heart may be enlightened
> so you may know what is the hope of His calling,
> what are the glorious riches of His inheritance
> among the saints, and what is the immeasurable
> greatness of His power to us who believe, according
> to the working of His vast strength. (Eph. 1:17–19)

Now perk up your ears! Paul's about to tell you what kind of glorious power is available to you for having a positive attitude toward cleaning bathrooms, cooking meals, shopping for groceries, making a speech, taking care of family and friends, and for *anything* in your life that calls you to exert mental, emotional, and physical strength! "He demonstrated this power in the Messiah by raising Him from the dead and seating Him at His right hand in the heavens" (Eph. 1:20).

Now I want you to grab hold of this. The Word of God says that, with Jesus Christ living in me, I have power to do *anything*, and it's the same power that God used when he raised Jesus from the dead! This includes having power for a positive attitude!

I remember when that reality first sank in with me years ago. I was teaching about the power of God, using the Ephesians text. All of a sudden the Holy Spirit seemed to whoosh (as only the Holy Spirit can) over me with the truth that I didn't have to dread cleaning the week's worth of mess in my house because I had the power of God to get me through it, and I could still smile when I finished! Right during the middle of my speech that day, God spoke to my heart saying, "I'm all you need to have the positive attitude I want you to have. And this positive attitude is available right in the middle of all the negative things filling your life!"

Friend, what is there in your life that the *power of the living God* cannot handle?

I pray that you will be filled with a fresh new insight about how your heavenly Father longs to help you and get you through the rough moments of your day. And he especially wants to be a part of all the areas you've never considered giving to him—areas like laundry, garbage, telephone calls, cleaning your desk at the office, and attending those long meetings!

God in all his practical and positive power longs to share it with his children. I took him up on his offer years ago, and for me, cleaning the bathroom in my own strength is a thing of the past!

- ☞ Are there areas in your life where you'd like to experience the power of God as described in Ephesians 1?

- ☞ Are you willing to believe that he will empower you with his positive attitude?

Chapter Nine

The Gift of His Power

"And what is the immeasurable greatness of His power to us who believe, according to the working of His vast strength."
EPHESIANS 1:19

You've been reading about the availability of God's power. As his children we have the gift of accessing his power in every situation we face, including our daily attitudes! The power available for you to have a positive attitude is the same power God used when he raised Christ from the dead. How powerful is that?

And what's your part in accessing this mighty power? The "us who believe" phrase in the Ephesians verse refers to those of us who have trusted Jesus Christ to be our Lord and Savior. We believe in the resurrected Son of God who died for our sins, dying a substitutionary death for our sins so that we will not be separated from God. We believe he is now sitting at the right hand of God waiting for us to live with him throughout all eternity.

It's almost mind-boggling to think that all we have to do to tap into God's power to give us a positive attitude is to *believe*. But you see, dear friend, Jesus already did the hard part; that's why our part is only to *believe*. And because

I have trusted him as my Savior, I can also trust him to help me find a positive attitude.

Also, it still thrills me to know that God not only saved me for eternal life with him after I die, but he saved me for *now*, while I'm here living this life. I don't have to wait until eternity to experience his tremendous power, joy, and love. I can experience it now, right here on earth, while I'm living, breathing, being frazzled on many days. His presence in me is what I need to have a positive attitude. I certainly can't experience it through my own effort on most days.

This means I can believe God for a positive attitude in my relationships with my family, as well as believe him for a positive attitude at work, in running errands, and even while trying to finish up everything before I go to bed at night. I have the positive attitude of Jesus Christ living inside of me to make me positive about everything!

And remember the first step to being positive is to determine to think positively! It's a matter of choice, an act of will.

Without believing that I have that power and then accessing it, I tend to fall prey to whining and complaining. We live in a much less than perfect world. In fact, as stated earlier, it's more natural to behave in negative ways than in positive ones. We are born with a sinful nature, and not until we invite Jesus into our hearts do we have the opportunity of his positive spirit guiding us. The opportunity and challenge come in *choosing* to be positive in a negative world. Only God can provide that positive attitude when daily living is filled with so much stress. He provides it but allows us the opportunity to choose it!

At times I intellectually grasp a concept, but I can't quite plug it in to my way of doing things. I find it so frustrating to understand what God is saying and yet remain uncertain as to how to put it to work in my life. I mean, I know that he wants me to have a positive attitude, but in some areas it's just hard to understand how to be positive. Again, that's when I turn to Scripture and *pray*!

"Help me understand Your instruction, and I will obey it and follow it with all my heart" (Ps. 119:34).

When I pray that prayer, God gradually—or sometimes immediately—begins to show me how to be more positive. You can be assured that God will always answer when you call out to him. He will impress upon your heart what words to say or which way to go. As you seek him and long to hear from him, remember he longs to speak to you and fill you with his presence.

When you're anxious about something, it's difficult to feel positive. Anxious feelings can multiply rapidly, causing you to become focused on them, then preoccupied with them, unless you keep them in check. Anxiety and worry can lead to an extremely negative attitude. Before I put positive thinking on my daily to-do list, I remember often waking up in the morning and becoming so absorbed in all that I had to accomplish that day that I was worn out from running before I ever got out of bed.

The enemy used worry to make me become self-absorbed, keeping me distracted about the positive power of God. The devil doesn't want me to have a positive outlook and a life that glorifies God, so he tempts me to focus on me!

Years ago, after praying about the worries that were occupying my mind and stealing my peace, the Lord gave me this strategy. I found a small box and named it my WORRY BOX. Then I wrote on slips of paper the worries that were occupying my mind and robbing me of his peace and joy. I placed each slip of paper in the box, committing not to worry about them for an entire week. I was instantly amazed at the freedom I experienced. It was proof to me that by worrying I was not resolving the situations, only increasing the emotional turmoil inside of me.

As I continued this practice of creating worry-free weeks, a wonderful benefit became apparent. Often by the end of the week, the worry had taken care of itself, or at least didn't seem nearly as harassing. And for the big issues, even though I had to continue to deal with them, I experienced a break from the worry that was attached to them.

His positive power is also available for tasks that irritate you. A lot of times this irritation spills over to the people behind them. Many women experience major frustration (that's mildly said) at the end of the day when they are already tired and worn out and have to clean a dirty house. When that happens to me, I choose once again to focus on Scripture! "And whatever you do, in word or in deed, do everything in the name of the Lord Jesus, giving thanks to God the Father through Him" (Col. 3:17).

Honestly sometimes as I'm praying that prayer, I begin laughing. The intensity of my irritation determines the number of times I speak, sigh, or shout this Scripture. If you are truly determined to get God's positive attitude to burst within you, then you won't stop until you become positive!

I smile when I think about the young mother of three little boys who came up to me after a recent Frazzled Female session. I had been teaching about how God wants us to talk to him about everything in our lives, especially about those many irritations that fill our days. She said, "God doesn't want me to talk to him about the underwear my little boys scatter through the house."

My reply: "Oh, yes, he does!"

Dear friend, does God want you to experience peace of mind? Does he want you to have a positive outlook on life, one that leaves you feeling energized with his power living inside of you? Does he want you to be free from the worry and negativity that is robbing your joy? Oh, yes, he does!

Feel encouraged as you take the tiny baby steps of growing a more positive attitude. Life's hard, and being positive requires desire and persistence. But remember, you have a loving heavenly Father who is taking notice of you and is cheering you on as you turn your heart and thoughts toward him.

- Have you ever thought of having a positive attitude as being a determined choice?

- Do you have worries that you can place in a "worry box"?

Chapter Ten

Being Positive in Negative Circumstances

"Search for the LORD and for His strength;
seek His face always."
PSALM 105:4

No way! Glenda thought as she read her devotional about being positive in the midst of trials. The author challenged her at the very point of her vulnerability. She had been engaged a year ago to a man she desperately loved and longed to spend her life with. Three weeks before the wedding, he walked away pledging his love to another. Glenda had experienced a wide range of intense emotions, and none of them were positive! From shock to anger to confusion and finally rejection, she had sunk as low as anyone could sink. How could she possibly see anything positive about this horrible situation that left her extremely cynical and negative!

During the writing of this book, I received a phone call from a friend who was also experiencing difficulty with the concept of being positive when her world was falling apart. "It doesn't seem humanly possible," she said, "to be positive when so many bad things are happening to me. It doesn't seem realistic," were her words.

God understands our inability and even our resistance to being positive when everything inside us feels negative. He knows that in our weakness we are not able to overlook all of life's negatives and immediately jump into a positive lifestyle. He doesn't want us to ignore the facts of the negative situation, but he does want us to rely on his power to get us through one step at a time.

Again, I remind you that sometimes you have to fight to be victorious with that positive attitude. It's a choice you make. Remember positive Abraham in chapter 6? His arsenal was filled with exactly what you and I have; God and the ability to choose.

> Against hope, with hope he believed, so that he
> became the father of many nations, according to
> what had been spoken: So will your descendants be.
> He considered his own body to be already dead
> (since he was about a hundred years old), and the
> deadness of Sarah's womb, without weakening in
> the faith. He did not waver in unbelief at God's
> promise, but was strengthened in his faith and gave
> glory to God, because he was fully convinced that
> what He had promised He was also able to perform.
> (Rom. 4:18–21)

Abraham believed God not because things made sense, but because he knew God would and could do what he said he would do even though Abraham had reason not to believe. But I imagine, considering the condition of his and Sarah's body, this was not an easy choice. I'm sure that Abraham had fighting moments at times, where he had to strengthen his resolve and *determine* to believe that God would do what he said he would do. And you know, God continued to bless Abraham for his hope and positive attitude.

God will continue to bless you for hoping in him and for striving to keep your attitude positive. And by the way, being positive doesn't necessarily mean that you are happy. *Life does not always make us happy!* And being a Christian does not make you immune to the trials and troubles of life. I want you to realize that being happy and being positive are not the same thing. Even when we are not happy, we can be positively confident that God is in control of our lives and we have the ultimate victory over all of life's negatives in Jesus Christ!

As Christians we have a reason to be positive. We have a positive God! And sometimes God may ask you to be positive and hopeful about a situation simply because he is God and he is in charge of your life. The world says, "Seeing is believing." But the Bible says for us to "(trust in, adhere to, and rely on) God" (Rom. 4:24 AMP). And many times that's when we "don't see" the outcome.

In thinking about a positive versus a negative attitude, maybe you've heard someone say (or you've thought this yourself): *I'm not being negative; I'm just being realistic.* Some people think being positive is not being realistic. That line of thinking is contrary to Scripture. Just like Abraham, you can face each situation by choosing to place your faith and hope in God. As you practice this, you will develop a mind-set that is open to the will of God, whatever that may be.

Consider Glenda, whose fiancé ran out on her. By adopting a negative attitude, Glenda might say, "My life is over. No one will ever want me again. I'm going to be miserable the rest of my life." By being positive and realistic, Glenda could say, "I hate that this happened, and I hurt so much. I know it's going to take time to get through this, but I trust God to restore me. He may send someone else my way if that's his will for me. God knows what's best for my life now and in the future."

Whether you realize it or not, day after day messages are being encoded in your mind. You carry on conversations with yourself, interpret situations, and cast judgments. This self-talk can either be explosive and filled with doubt and criticism or positive and filled with hope.

Here are some examples of self-talk:

Why don't I just give up?

God is in control. Things are going to work out somehow.

I don't understand, but I trust him.

God must really be disappointed in me.

I'm never going to make it through this.

Father, I turn this over to you. I choose to believe you will take care of me.

Along with self-talk, there's also the talk of others influencing you. You may have grown up in an environment filled with negativity. There may be those in your life who are continuing to fill you with criticism and gloom. Remember, you are responsible to God in your relationship with him. To be successful in your attitude and in your life, you must not take on the negative spirit of those around you. This is all about *you and God!* If you ask him, he will begin to help you lay the negative comments of others to rest.

I am now choosing and training myself to focus on my heavenly Father right in the middle of negative talk and circumstances. It's a continual choice, and sometimes it's difficult. But God in his love and grace is helping me along the way and blessing me by offering his continual energy, forgiveness, and power to turn the hopelessly negative into powerful and positive moments with him!

OK. It's time to move forward with your newly acquired positive thinking skills and step right into the negative mama of them all—NO TIME! I'm excited for you to take a few more of those baby steps. Keep goin' girl! Your little steps are leading you closer to the heart of God!

- Could you be more positive about situations that do not make you happy?

- Is your mind mostly filled with positive self-talk or negative self-talk?

PART THREE

I Don't Have Enough Time!

"Be still and know that I am God."
PSALM 46:10 NIV

With tons of time management programs, tips, and strategies available to help us more effectively use our precious minutes, why is it at the end of the day we still throw up our hands and cry out, "I just don't have enough time!"

Actually, God spoke to me about this particular issue in a really specific way when I was putting together a seminar on time management. What he revealed to me seemed so simple that I couldn't believe I had missed this truth for so long. After consistently trying out my "new plan" from him, I have not only become more time efficient but more peaceful instead of running consistently at a breakneck speed to get everything done and marked off my daily to-do list.

He revealed his time management plan with this Scripture: "'Bring the full 10 percent into the storehouse so that there may be food in My house. Test Me in this way,' says the LORD of Hosts. 'See if I will not open the floodgates of

heaven and pour out a blessing for you without measure'"
(Mal. 3:10).

I sensed him telling me that this verse applies not only to
the money I give to him but also to the way I give him my
time! I got excited as I realized he was saying that if I spent
time with him every single day, then he would open the floodgates of heaven and pour out his blessings on my life.

The principle is this. God desires a relationship with
you. And he desires daily communication that includes worship, prayer, and Scripture study. And when you give him
your time, he showers his *love* and *peace* and *joy* throughout
your day. The things you do become more God centered and
less frenetic. He takes your time and multiplies it with his
blessings. You don't actually have more time, but it seems like
you do.

Begin to imagine a lifestyle of less huffing and puffing
and more calmness and fulfillment. When you recognize that
God is in control of your time, you actually get the things done
in a day that you need to get done! It can happen and *will
happen if you put God's time before your time.*

Chapter Eleven

God Is in Control

"He must increase, but I must decrease."
JOHN 3:30

God had given Jochebed, the mother of Moses, the gift of a beautiful baby boy, yet Pharaoh had ordered the death of every Hebrew male baby. How overwhelming her circumstances must have seemed! The mother of Moses knew God. Knowing him led her to trust him to take care of her child. Hebrews 11:23 tells us she disobeyed the king by hiding Moses for three months. What a courageous act of faith to place her baby in the bulrushes at the river's edge. As a woman who loved God and understood the yearning of her own heart, Jochebed trusted him completely with the welfare of her child. Her faith was rewarded as God inclined the heart of Pharaoh's daughter to save the child, making his mother his nursemaid.

> Now a man from the family of Levi married a
> Levite woman. The woman became pregnant and
> gave birth to a son; when she saw that he was beau-
> tiful, she hid him for three months. But when she
> could no longer hide him, she got a papyrus basket
> for him and coated it with asphalt and pitch. She

placed the child in it and set it among the reeds by
the bank of the Nile. Then his sister stood at a distance in order to see what would happen to him.

Pharaoh's daughter went down to bathe at the
Nile while her servant girls walked along the river-
bank. Seeing the basket among the reeds, she sent
her slave girl to get it. When she opened it, she saw
the child—a little boy, crying. She felt sorry for him
and said, "This is one of the Hebrew boys."

Then his sister said to Pharaoh's daughter,
"Should I go and call a woman from the Hebrews to
nurse the boy for you?"

"Go." Pharaoh's daughter told her. So the girl
went and called the boy's mother. Then Pharaoh's
daughter said to her, "Take this child and nurse
him for me, and I will pay your wages." So the
woman took the boy and nursed him. When the
child grew older, she brought him to Pharaoh's
daughter, and he became her son. She named him
Moses, "Because," she said, "I drew him out of the
water." (Exod. 2:1–10)

Just imagine the intense emotions Jochebed must have felt
as she lowered her baby boy into the water! She certainly was
in the middle of an unsettling circumstance, yet she trusted
that God was in control.

It takes sheer discipline to trust God in the midst of unsettling circumstances. Feeling like you don't have enough time
to get everything done that needs to get done is definitely
unsettling and can leave you feeling extremely anxious about
life in general. It's frustrating and even exhausting just *trying*
to plan how to get meals fixed, the house cleaned, groceries
bought, people taken care of, not to mention the endless meetings, phone calls, and appointments that fill our days.

I'm sure Jochebed drew from her maternal instincts in
designing a plan she hoped would protect her baby. More

importantly, she drew strength from her God who led her through a mission to protect and preserve not only the life of her young child but an entire nation of God's children. How the Hebrew people would be blessed through the faithful leadership of Moses! Through Jochebed's example we can learn two important principles of time management. First, Jochebed relied on God. Second, she was persistent. Her firm faith gave her the strength she needed to do what God called her to do.

Do you need more time in your life to exercise or plan nutritious meals? What about more time to build family relationships or show kindness to neighbors? Maybe you just need a little more relaxation time and time to do something just for you!

It takes tremendous faith, discipline, and persistence to manage your time God's way. Perhaps it's time for you to seek his counsel about what you do with the time he has given you. I bet if you put him first, he'll do for you just as he did for Jochebed and what he's doing for me—reward you with his strength, his joy, and his provision. In fact, I'm sure he will!

- ☞ Are you running short on energy and low on time?

- ☞ Have you considered asking God to help you manage your time?

Chapter Twelve

More . . .

"God, create a clean heart for me and
renew a steadfast spirit within me."
PSALM 51:10

Betty read in the Sunday church bulletin that a ladies' Bible study would begin next week. Her heart jumped with excitement as she anticipated gathering with Christian women to study and talk about Scripture. She longed to grow in her relationship with the Lord. She wanted to experience his peace and joy in her life on a daily basis.

By Thursday night, Betty was exhausted from working at her daily job and coming home to begin "second shift" (the title she gave her responsibilities at home). Once again, she shelved the idea of the Bible study, feeling she didn't have enough time. She would attend when life wasn't so busy.

Oh my! Can't we all identify with Betty; longing to grow in our relationship with the Lord so that we can experience his joy and peace but just not having enough time to do so?

Having a quiet time with our heavenly Father so that we can grow that love relationship doesn't scream at us the way daily life does. It's so easy to put off that time with him, convincing ourselves that it will be easier to spend time with him when life isn't so hectic.

Women often ask me if it's OK to have their daily quiet time while driving to work or getting ready in the morning or while doing a number of other things throughout the day but focusing on God while they're busy doing these things.

My answer: *Yes, but first . . .*

Yes! God so longs for you to invite him into the midst of all your busyness. He wants you to have a lifestyle of being aware of him and consulting him during every part of your day.

But first, it is my strong belief based on personal experience that I cannot tune into God and be totally aware of him as I go through my day unless I have *first* had my quiet and personal time with him. This is a time when I focus exclusively on my love for him, worshipping him, seeking his guidance, reading and meditating on Scripture. Sure I can do these things while driving or cooking meals or getting ready for work, but I can't do them without being somewhat distracted.

God longs for your undivided attention. Multitasking with God is not focusing exclusively on him! He honors your effort and blesses you beyond imagination when you dedicate time just for him while doing nothing else. I'm reminded of the time when my boys were little. If I tried to do something else when I was sitting on the floor playing with them, they would grab my face to get my attention and look me straight in the eyes and say, "Play, Mommy, play!"

Now God is not going to grab you and make you stop everything to spend time with him, but he wants you to. He's allowing you to make that choice. And maybe you don't have a lot of time to do this each day, but don't you have *some* time?

The benefit, you see, is that in offering God some of your time exclusively each day, he will bless you beyond measure. By sitting still with him and becoming comfortable in what "still" feels like, you will be better able to still yourself in him when troubling times hit. If you've never been still with God, then how will you be still with him when the rug is pulled out from under you and you desperately need to feel his still calmness invading your circumstances and saturating you with his peace?

It is from that still and quiet place that I have learned to take him from there into the noisiness of life. After my early morning quiet time, then, yes, I do worship him as I drive, as I get ready for work, and as I move throughout my day. But in order to experience him in those "other places," I have to go to the "quiet place" first. Honestly, for me, it just won't work any other way.

Liza shared this experience with her Frazzled Female Bible study group: "When I walked into my kitchen at 6:00 a.m., I looked at the dirty dishes in the sink and then at my Bible. For a moment I was torn about what to do. Doing the dishes would give me a head start on my day, but I wouldn't have time for Bible study. I decided to read my Bible. I had the most wonderful experience with God. The rest of my day went smoothly because I was filled with his peace."

That's exactly what God wants to show you. Remember what he said in that Malachi verse? "Test Me in this way. . . . See if I will not open the floodgates of heaven and pour out a blessing for you without measure" (Mal. 3:10).

He's calling me. He's calling you. He's calling all of his children to a quiet and loving and deeply personal relationship with him. He wants you to test him in this so that he can show you all the blessings he longs to shower upon your life as you gradually learn to love him more and more.

And no, you will not have more time, but the time you have will be more! I can't explain it, but I know it's true! And so do many other women who have taken on this challenge of giving God their time and attention first thing in the morning before tackling the chores of the day.

Perhaps this is a testing ground for you. God is longing for you to "test him in this" so that he may "open the floodgates and pour out a blessing for you without measure."

- ☞ Have you ever felt like you just don't have time to grow your relationship with the Lord?

- ☞ Would you like to experience the floodgates of heaven opening and pouring out blessings on you?

Chapter Thirteen

The Core of the Problem

"Turn my eyes from looking at what is worthless;
give me life in Your ways."
PSALM 119:37

Emily managed to get away from her family to attend a women's retreat for the weekend. As she sat in a crowded auditorium with other women who shared the same frustrations of having too much to do and too little time, she heard these words: "God will not bless you in doing the things he has not called you to do—even if they're *good* things." Emily was stunned. Her life was full of good things. Could it be God didn't want her to do all these things?

Take a look at the following list of "good" things.

- Teaching Sunday school
- Serving on a committee
- Volunteering in school
- Singing in the choir
- Tutoring
- Belonging to a civic club
- Visiting the elderly

Oh, such a small sampling, but you get the idea. And you could add a lot of other examples from your own life, I'm sure. In fact, I know many women who have filled their lives with way too many good things! Many Christian women, swallowed up in an endless array of duties, responsibilities, and service, miss out on God's best for them. This plethora of activity often steals their creativity, their playtime, their joy, and leaves them physically, emotionally, mentally, and spiritually depleted.

God has a beautiful invitation to all who find themselves caught up in the lifestyle of *too many things to do with not enough time to do them.* Through Isaiah, God issues an invitation to all who are thirsty, to all who are not satisfied with life, to all who are too busy to enjoy his peace and joy.

> Come, everyone who is thirsty, come to the waters; . . . Seek the LORD while He may be found; call to Him while He is near. . . . "For My thoughts are not your thoughts, and your ways are not My ways. For as heaven is higher than earth, so My ways are higher than your ways, and My thoughts than your thoughts." (Isa. 55:1a, 6, 8–9)

I assure you if you are anxious, pressured, and depleted by the demands placed on your life right now, God has something better in mind for you. Too little time is not actually the problem. The core of the problem may be having too much to do! And through accepting the invitation of the Lord to come to him, he will give you his thoughts about the scheduling of your time!

God does not want you to do every good thing. I can't tell you which things you should be doing, but he can. That's why you must check his thinking and seek his counsel in everything you do. Isaiah admonishes us to seek the Lord and consider his thoughts and ways. He alone can tell you what you need to be involved in during this time in your life.

I know it may sound a bit cut and dried at first, this notion of just asking God what you should be doing and waiting for him to tell you, but, friend, it's true! If you offer your heart, mind, and emotions to your heavenly Father, he will direct you about all the things he wants you to be involved in during your daily schedule.

For me, the revelation about what should occupy my days comes in my quiet alone time. Part of what I do during that time with him is go over my plans for the day, praying over each item and asking his take on what fills my day. He, more than once, has impressed me to strike something off my list.

I've learned not to assume that just because something is good, God wants me to be doing it at this particular time in my life. Thinking about it, everything I do could be classified as "good"—from visiting in the nursing home to serving on committees at church to checking in on neighbors. I can't, however, do *all* of those good things *all of the time.*

When I seek God's counsel and ask him to be in control of my to-do list, he truly impresses on me what should be on it in the first place. Sometimes I'm impressed to strike off "little things." There have been other times when he has called me specifically to drop out of an activity for a while so that I may have more time to be with my family and grow our relationships.

For instance, after the birth of my second child, I was seeking God's guidance about being the mom he wanted me to be. He clearly impressed on me to refrain from night meetings during the first year of my baby's life. Now I have to tell you it's rare that the Lord has been so specific about "what to do" down to the time element. But that particular event was one of those times. I was obedient to what I knew he had told me to do and stepped away from all activities that caused me to be away from home at night for the first year after Lane's birth.

That "baby" is nineteen years old now, and I can look back on that situation and know that it was a blessing to move in the direction of my Father's leadership. I still don't know fully why God gave such a clear admonition in this. He did not lead that way when my older son was born and does not lead many other women in the same way, but for me he knew that this was best. I trusted him then, and I trust him now to be in control of what fills my days.

I believe God wants us to learn to enjoy his fellowship at a more relaxed pace. For some reason we busy women equate being busy for God as being productive for him. But you know, he is showing me that I'm more productive when I'm less busy and more relaxed.

It's my prayer that you will begin to check areas in your life where you might be overcommitted. Take some time with the Lord, seeking his direction. And remember, making sure you are less busy will help you have more time for sitting at his feet, and that's to your advantage!

"There is need of only one or but a few things. Mary has chosen the good portion [that which is to her advantage]" (Luke 10:42 AMP).

- ☞ Are you doing too many good things?

- ☞ Are you willing to take the activities in your life to the Lord, asking him to reveal to you what you should be doing at this time in your life?

Chapter Fourteen

Blessed by God

Who can find a capable wife? She is far more precious than jewels. The heart of her husband trusts in her, and he will not lack anything good. She rewards him with good, not evil, all the days of her life. . . . Strength and honor are her clothing, and she can laugh at the time to come. She opens her mouth with wisdom, and loving instruction is on her tongue. She watches over the activities of her household and is never idle. Her sons rise up and call her blessed. Her husband also praises her: "Many women are capable, but you surpass them all!" Charm is deceptive and beauty is fleeting, but a woman who fears the Lord will be praised.

PROVERBS 31:10–12, 25–30

Sue's heart sank as she considered the description of the virtuous woman in Proverbs 31. She had recommitted her life to God, asking him to show her how to be the woman he wanted her to be. She also asked him to show her how to get everything done on a daily basis, glorifying him in the process. She was flooded with feelings of guilt and self-doubt as she read through the qualities of God's ideal woman.

Do you ever compare yourself to other women? At times God may give you an example in another woman. He may speak to you through her words or lifestyle, drawing you to his character through what you see in her. However, at other times, *you* may initiate the comparison, and the focus becomes jealousy and self-pity because you can't seem to "measure up."

Let's take a look at that virtuous woman of Proverbs 31. Here's my paraphrase:

> She was up before dawn.
> She had her own garden.
> She made clothes for herself and her family.
> She owned and ran her own business.
> She was a wonderful homemaker.
> Her husband praised her.
> Her children adored her.
> She was intelligent.
> She took care of the physical needs of her family.
> She spoke with wisdom.
> She helped others.
> She was in shape—physically, mentally, emotionally, spiritually.
> She feared God.

Well, what do you think? Any possibility of your getting a close comparison?

Now before you toss out this chapter, let me answer for you with a resounding YES! You *can* become the ideal woman. Not because of what you can do but because of who God is!

When I scan that list of descriptives, one quality towers head and shoulders above the rest. Do you know which one?

She feared God.

The phrase in Proverbs from the Amplified Bible reads, she *worshipfully feared the Lord.* In other words, she worshipped God and put him at the top of her priority list. Only one thing is mentioned in Proverbs 31:10 as making her value "far above rubies" (KJV), and that's her spiritual life. It *all* goes back to sitting at the feet of Jesus!

As you worship him, read his Word, and seek his counsel, God will tell you what things should be part of your life. Planting your garden may be sowing seeds of kindness through a volunteer project or maybe showing particular interest in a family member's activities. Being a wonderful homemaker may be offering daily encouragement to your husband or listening to your child pour out frustrations about friendships. It's accomplishing many things by first doing the one thing, and that's making time with God top priority!

You will also be strengthened mentally, emotionally, and physically as you make time with God your top priority. Be affirmed and encouraged, dear sister. God longs for you to experience peace in your daily activities. He wants your life to be filled with joy, not turmoil and panic. And to that end he is inviting you to the place of ultimate comfort, rest, fulfillment, and excitement: his presence!

Are you catching the point of what all of this has to do with your time management issues? There's simply no better way to take control of your time than by *choosing to give your time to God!* In seeking his direction about your daily schedule and all the things that take up your day, you are inviting him to be a part of every element of how you spend your time. Taking time to do that will result in blessings on your life that you simply can't experience any other way!

- ☞ Can you think of a godly woman who exhibits God's peace and joy?

- ☞ Is a personal relationship with Jesus a priority in her life?

PART FOUR

People Are Getting on My Nerves!

"But thanks be to God, who gives us the victory through our Lord Jesus Christ!"
1 CORINTHIANS 15:57

OK. Let's bring it down to gut-level honesty here. Can't people just drive you crazy?

Years ago I was in the mountains of North Carolina, leading the administrative staff and congregation of a small church through a team-building session. We were exploring the strengths and weaknesses of various behavior styles, highlighting the differences of each. Volunteers from the audience represented each style of behavior. It surprised us all when one mild-mannered deacon erupted on the spot, "I just can't stand people like that!"

Truth is, there are just days when people can get on your last nerve! Since we will be living alongside others as long as we breathe on this earth, it's important to examine spiritual strategies to help us deal with all the people Jesus loves, including the ones who rub us the wrong way.

> Be in agreement with one another. . . . Do not repay anyone evil for evil. Try to do what is honorable in everyone's eyes. . . . Friends, do not avenge yourselves; instead, leave room for His wrath.
> (Rom. 12:16–19)

67

Chapter Fifteen

Living Peacefully

"Lord, set up a guard for my mouth; keep watch
at the door of my lips."
PSALM 141:3

A few words spoken by another can throw you off track and disrupt your peace. Jesus' words had this effect on his disciples as he prepared them for his heavenly departure.

"Your heart must not be troubled. Believe in God; believe also in Me. In My Father's house are many dwelling places; if not, I would have told you. I am going away to prepare a place for you. If I go away and prepare a place for you, I will come back and receive you to Myself, so that where I am you may be also. You know the way where I am going."

"Lord," Thomas said, "we don't know where You're going. How can we know the way?"

Jesus told him, "I am the way, the truth, and the life. No one comes to the Father except through Me." (John 14:1–6)

Can you imagine the surprise, the confusion, and the fear that the disciples must have experienced at the words of Jesus? They had left everything to follow him, and now he told them he was going away. He was actually leaving them! I believe they desperately wanted to understand, but more than that, they wanted the answer to the question that was lodged in their pounding hearts, "But what about us?"

Self lies at the heart of many problems we face in dealing with people. We want to know, *Why are you telling me this? What am I supposed to do? How should I feel? Who is going to help me? Why don't you understand me? Don't you care about me? What's going to happen to me?*

Consider Sharon who works in an office with five other people. They often have lunch together and chat during breaks. Sharon recently realized that Alesa is acting differently toward her. She seldom speaks, and when she does, it's with a condescending tone. Alesa's unfriendly attitude is beginning to bother Sharon. She wonders, *Why are you treating me this way? What happened to our friendship? What can I do to make everything OK?*

I'm like Sharon. My style of behavior is one that enjoys interacting with people. So when people say things and behave in ways that I don't understand, I can be easily hurt, confused, and offended! It's an ongoing challenge for me to accept and apply the *peace of Jesus* when I encounter difficulty with what others say and how they behave.

John 14:27 is a comforting verse that is often quoted in funeral or memorial services. It has also given me great insight to experiencing the peace and comfort of Jesus in "people" situations. "Peace I leave with you. My peace I give to you. I do not give to you as the world gives. Your heart must not be troubled or fearful" (John 14:27).

I often allow the words and behaviors of others to confuse and unsettle me. I believe Jesus is saying to me through this verse that I don't have to be troubled, afraid, agitated, intimidated, or unsettled in any area of my life. He has given me his peace!

It's a good thing to recognize unsettled feelings, but it's not productive to get self-absorbed in the process. And when you get caught up in the "me aspect" when you're experiencing trying times with others, then you can quickly become self-absorbed.

However, when you shift your focus from self to the peace that Jesus offers, you open the door to understanding by getting self out of the way. And friend, getting *self* out of the way removes a huge barrier to understanding! And the good news is that you don't have to shift this focus in your own strength and by your own efforts. You have a personal trainer standing right by your side who will pick up that heavy weight of self, set it aside, and reposition your focus. He's waiting for you to ask for his help!

If you have invited Jesus to live in your heart, then your helper, the Holy Spirit, dwells within you, ready to energize you with the peace of Jesus! For me, his peace rushes in to settle my whirling and random thoughts. And then I'm energized with a new focus. It's a focus not on self but on the ways of Jesus.

I'm training my self mentally to step back from the negative feelings, asking the Holy Spirit to take over my mind and emotions. My "people problems" are gradually providing more and more opportunities to experience the peace of Jesus! And you know what? That's a pretty exciting thing!

"And I will ask the Father, and He will give you another Counselor to be with you forever" (John 14:16).

- ☞ Are you experiencing difficulty with another person or a group of people?

- ☞ Would shifting your focus from *self* to the *peace of Jesus* help you deal with others?

Chapter Sixteen

It Depends on Me!

"For by the grace given to me, I tell everyone among you not to
think of himself more highly than he should think. Instead,
think sensibly, as God has distributed a measure of faith to each
one. Now as we have many parts in one body, and all the
parts do not have the same function, in the same way we who
are many are one body in Christ and individually members
of one another. . . . Show family affection to one another with
brotherly love. Outdo one another in showing honor."

ROMANS 12:3–5, 10

These words are part of a personal letter from Paul to the
church in Rome. I enjoy Paul's writings immensely. He
just has a way of laying things out! People are different and he
addresses those differences. We may have different spiritual
gifts, different behavioral styles, and different ideas of right
and wrong. But Paul encourages believers in Jesus to reach out
aggressively to others through Christ's love, regardless of the
differences.

Reaching out with the love of Christ can sometimes be
challenging because differences often breed conflict. I was in
earshot recently of a verbal conflict where tensions and heart
rates were escalating. The disagreement was over the best way

to handle a memo that had come into that particular office. To me, an innocent bystander (and happy to be one), this conflict was a perfect example of how two people with two points of view can each be right, but each one thinks her way is the only way!

Truly, many conflicts could be avoided if we simply stepped back, took a deep breath (or three or four), and conceded our right to be right. I realize that conceding our right to be right and getting rid of *self* is a slow and ongoing process. But for me there's peace in even taking little baby steps in this direction. I know that when I become preoccupied with *my* way, *my* feelings, *my* rights, then my energy is drained and my peace slips away. But when I make a conscious and deliberate choice to *put me out of the way*, then I can more easily turn the situation over to Jesus and let him handle it.

And that's basically how I do it. I slow down and say aloud if the circumstance permits, "I'm moving *self* out of the way. Jesus, please take over this situation!"

As simple as that sounds, that's just what you do. You *choose* to stop focusing on your feelings and your rights and force yourself to put the other person's viewpoint above your own. This is often a difficult thing for me to do. But with persistence and determination, it's becoming an easier choice!

It's particularly difficult when your "self feelings" are justified. You may have been treated unfairly or unkindly. Getting rid of self depends on your degree of hurt. It may help you to remember this. By giving up self, you are in no way justifying the other person's behavior. You are simply following the commands given in Scripture to "bless those who persecute you; bless and do not curse. . . . Do not repay anyone evil for evil. Try to do what is honorable in everyone's eyes. If possible, on your part, live at peace with everyone" (Rom. 12:14, 17–18).

I remember years ago being so frustrated about trash that was left lying around in our yard after the cans had been emptied on trash pickup day. Week after week I had carefully secured each bag, hoping all the contents would make it to the trash bin instead of being scattered throughout the yard. Finally it occurred to me to show a little appreciation for the trash service instead of being concerned with the remnants. I mean, *most* of it was making it to the truck! With great care I painted a sign and plastered it on the outside of our two backyard garbage cans. It read, "I appreciate you for carrying off my trash." That was the last time trash was scattered across our yard.

I learned a valuable lesson that day. That incident helped me learn how to deal with people in my life who frustrate me. A little appreciation and kindness go a long way. And since that time I've considered frustrating circumstances as opportunities to put self aside, practice his love, and experience his peace.

"Show family affection to one another with brotherly love. Outdo one another in showing honor" (Rom. 12:10).

- ☞ Is there someone in your life who could use a little appreciation and kindness?

- ☞ Can you think of a way to show that appreciation and kindness?

Chapter Seventeen

This Is My Part

"Do not conform any longer to the pattern of this world, but be transformed by the renewing of your mind."

ROMANS 12:2 NIV

Several weeks ago I was eating lunch with a friend. When the server brought a basket with three rolls in it, my friend remarked, "Why would she bring three rolls for two people? Does she want us to have it out over the third one?"

Now I can tell you straight up that the world's way would be to fight it out! You know, stand up for yourself and take care of number one. But according to Colossians 3, that's not God's way. "Set your minds on what is above, not on what is on the earth" (v. 2).

In Paul's letter to the Colossians, he gives encouragement and something for the reader to hang on to. Then he fills this letter with practical applications for how we should live.

Therefore, God's chosen ones, holy and loved, put on heartfelt compassion, kindness, humility, gentleness, and patience, accepting one another and forgiving one another if anyone has a complaint against another. Just as the Lord has forgiven you, so also you must forgive. Above all, put on love—the perfect bond of unity. And let the peace of the Messiah, to which you were also called in one body, control your hearts. Be thankful. Let the message about the Messiah dwell richly among you, teaching and admonishing one another in all wisdom, and singing psalms, hymns, and spiritual songs, with gratitude in your hearts to God. And whatever you do, in word or in deed, do everything in the name of the Lord Jesus, giving thanks to God the Father through Him. (Col. 3:12–17)

A distinct connection exists between getting along with others and focusing on heaven. It's difficult, however, to set your mind on things above if you are being mistreated on earth, isn't it? Oh my, when those human emotions are aroused, it takes self-restraint to focus on heaven and behave with a heavenly mind-set!

For years I taught school. The years I spent in the middle-school classroom led to my belief that teenage girls have the market cornered on volatile relationships. HIGH VOLTAGE was the invisible sign hanging on my classroom door. Those girls just seemed wired to experience emotional pain, as well as dish it out. I loved them, and I loved teaching this age. It was a real challenge to dig through the layers of raging hormones and help them learn how to deal with the pressures of life (as well as learn some academics along the way).

Many walks to and from lunch and talks after school were spent on helping them understand that emotions can drive you nutty, and trying to figure out why people did things and said things was often wasted energy. I instructed them to write positive comments on a small tablet. They were to keep this tablet close by and refer to it often, rehearsing these lines so they could get used to saying them. Then when their feelings were hurt or they were treated unkindly, they were to retaliate with a kind and positive reaction instead of giving in to self-absorbed feelings that caused them to focus on how they had been hurt.

This strategy didn't always work, but it was a start at helping them redirect their thoughts from the immediate pain they were experiencing. They began to learn that they did have a choice to focus on something other than their hurt. And in the long run, there were less emotionally charged events to deal with on a daily basis.

Do you see how this strategy applies to focusing on things above when things on earth are getting you down? That *tablet of positive comments* is the Word of God. When people get you down by something they say or their behavior, pull a positive thought from God's Word and place it in your mind. Talk to the Lord about it. Say the Scripture along with your thoughts to him.

Lord, I'm trying to set my mind on what is above right now, not on what is going on here on earth. Help me to focus on you! Help me not to be absorbed with my own feelings but to focus on your peace and your love for this person. I know you want to help me. And I know you want me to be filled with your peace. By faith I'm choosing to focus on your love for this person instead of on my hurt.

Oh friend, don't you just long for the peace of Jesus to rule in your heart? I long for his peace in a mighty way. When I get ruffled or agitated, I'm determined I'm not going to stay that way. I keep going to the Lord with it, talking to him about the situation, and keeping it before him until I experience his peace.

As you become more intimate with the Savior, you *will* begin to experience his peace in indescribable ways. As you set aside a time each day to worship him, to thank him, to recognize him as the Lord of your thoughts, emotions, behavior, and your life, you will gradually move into a peaceful state of living. You'll find that as stress hits, your reaction will be softened and seasoned with God's grace. You'll begin to experience *freedom from self*. It's the gift of being in his presence. It's the gentleness of Jesus.

"Now the Lord is the Spirit; and where the Spirit of the Lord is, there is freedom" (2 Cor. 3:17).

- ☞ Can you think of a time you were hurt by someone's treatment of you?

- ☞ Would it have helped you to focus on "things above instead of things on earth?"

Chapter Eighteen

Loving Others

*"Be strong and courageous; don't be terrified or afraid
of them. For it is the LORD your God who goes with you;
He will not leave you or forsake you."*

DEUTERONOMY 31:6

A friend recently shared with me about how she and her
husband regularly meet with a group of friends for an
evening meal. On one particular occasion their friends
engaged in conversation with everyone at the table except
them. Ouch! Remembering times that I, too, have felt left out,
I hurt for my friend. And then I remembered Jesus' words to
his disciples. "I am going away to prepare a place for you"
(John 14:2).

Those words were not meant just for the disciples but for
us too! He's preparing a special place for us where there will
be no loneliness, no people competing with one another, no
hurt feelings, just harmony and acceptance in Jesus.

With Jesus living in your heart, you can look forward to a
grand celebration where you will be honored right alongside
Jesus. Just imagine! When you enter the marriage feast of the
Lamb, Jesus will be there. He is saving a place for you. John
was instructed to write these words recorded in the book of
Revelation.

Then I heard something like the voice of a vast multitude, like the sound of cascading waters, and like the rumbling of loud thunder, saying: Hallelujah—because our Lord God, the Almighty, has begun to reign! Let us be glad, rejoice, and give Him the glory, because the marriage of the Lamb has come, and His wife has prepared herself. She was permitted to wear fine linen, bright and pure. For the fine linen represents the righteous acts of the saints. Then he said to me, "Write: Blessed are those invited to the marriage feast of the Lamb!" (Rev. 19:6–9)

I imagine there will be much laughter and music and many conversations going on, but the King of kings and Lord of lords will offer *you* a special seat, as if you were the only one there. According to Revelation 2:17, Christ will give you a new name written on a white stone and only known to you and Him! "I will also give him a white stone, and on the stone a new name is inscribed that no one knows except the one who receives it." In other words, you and Jesus will be the perfectly at home together enjoying each other's company. Isn't that exciting and comforting?

You will never again feel left out, unwanted, or overlooked because Jesus himself will bring you into his presence and surround you with his love. Honestly, my friend, just focusing on this heavenly scene, knowing that it will last for eternity, helps me deal with the stress I face until then. When I look at "people" problems in this light, I can get through the difficult times because of Christ's love and the promise of spending forever with him.

Meanwhile, during the wait, here are some strategies that help me keep my focus. Perhaps you'll find them helpful too.

Make It Not Matter

Sometimes people do things that hurt us. When this happens to me, I pray, "Lord, just make it not matter to me." I have a tendency to get my feelings hurt easily. So when I am consumed with my self-pity, I pray this prayer and trust the Lord to lift the burden of self. And he gradually (and sometimes immediately) does.

Walk Away Before You Blow Up

If you feel your emotions soaring and your fuse lighting, remove yourself from the situation. This could mean ending a phone conversation or physically walking away from someone. This takes determination but is well worth the effort. When you calm down, you can think more clearly, and you will have time to talk to the Lord about it before you speak.

Breathe Deeply

If you begin to feel uncomfortable in a situation, take several deep breaths. This will help your blood and oxygen flow more freely to your brain and will help you think more clearly. And it's important that you think before you speak.

Deal with Your Negative Attitude Quickly

Don't allow negative thinking to find a home in your heart and mind. These disruptive thoughts can cause brain drain. Replace them with something positive like a Scripture verse or pleasant thought.

If You Are Wrong, Admit It Quickly

Admitting you are wrong shows your willingness to behave in a Christlike way. You model his compassion and forgiving nature as well.

John 15:3 states, "You are already clean because of the word I have spoken to you." In other words, you are clean with Jesus living inside of you. You are Jesus-clean even though there may be times when you feel covered in dirt because of how others are affecting you. I'm reminded of how I used to love to clean up my little boys after they had been outside playing. It never bothered me when they got covered in dirt from head to toe. I knew that dirt was temporary, and pretty soon those little bodies would shine after I scrubbed them clean. And to tell you the truth, I enjoyed the process. It was fun to see them all squeaky clean after they had gotten so dirty.

When Jesus Christ came to live in your heart, he cleaned you up and filled you with his righteousness. He knows your personality, and he knows the problems you experience. If you focus on him by worshipping him, loving him, and seeking his guidance, he will empower you to get along with others, no matter how difficult the process may be.

- ☞ Knowing that Jesus is empowering you and wants you to get along with others, is there someone with whom you can share the love of Jesus?

- ☞ Does being with Jesus for all eternity offer you comfort?

PART FIVE

Feeling Frazzled

"The LORD is near the brokenhearted;
He saves those crushed in spirit."
PSALM 34:18

Sometimes living just takes the life out of you, doesn't it? At best it seems that life is full of too many things to do, too many places to go, and too many people to take care of. It takes constant prodding and perseverance to keep things, situations, and people in some sort of orderly fashion. Well, this gal has noticed: ducks do *not* come in a row! And I can sure frazzle myself trying to get them to line up.

My friend Debbie called me yesterday afternoon. It was Friday, her day off. She works in an orthodontist's office Monday through Thursday and has the typical schedule of today's busy woman with a family to take care of, a job to work, and night meetings to attend. So Friday, her off-work day, is usually filled with more work than the other days. This is the catch-all day, the day that fills up with car repairs, doctors' appointments, housecleaning, bill paying—you get the picture.

Yesterday I caught the laughter in her voice as she said, "I took a nap this morning, right in the middle of everything I had to do, and it was wonderful!"

"You go, girl!"

That was my reaction to my friend's confession. The time has come for all frazzled females boldly to take back what has been taken from them—LIFE!

And friend, you have to determine to take care of yourself; to take time for *you.* It does not and will not come without effort because daily living is filled with too many pressures and things to do. I find that "taking time for self" is on the bottom of the list for most women I know.

Taking care of yourself and spending some time just enjoying life is preventive maintenance. It's a way of helping you become less frazzled and frenetic. It's also a wonderful gift to your family because you're nicer when you do something just for you!

Go ahead. Dream of something you love to do but never seem to have time for.

Need a jump-start? How about: take a relaxing bath, get a manicure, go for a leisurely walk, go to a movie with the girls, cuddle up with a good book, eat out, go shopping, or hike a trail, run a race, climb a mountain, soar on wings of eagles with new ideas of learning something new and exploring life in new ways. It's like finding the child within you who used to love to romp and play, anticipating snow and springtime and barefoot weather and birthday presents.

I strongly believe that life would be so much more enjoyable if we would just chill a little. We would not be as stressed out if we'd take more time to relax, exercise, eat properly, and enjoy God's gifts of celebration.

Now I know you're probably thinking, *How am I supposed to find the time to do this?* It starts in the mind. Just entertain the notion that possibly you *could* come up with one or two ways to take better care of yourself . . . and read on!

Chapter Nineteen

My House

"Therefore strengthen your tired hands and weakened knees,
and make straight paths for your feet, so that what is lame may
not be dislocated, but healed instead."
HEBREWS 12:12–13

It's only 8:00 a.m., but it already feels like afternoon to Janet! Before leaving for work at 6:30 this morning, she washed a load of clothes and got things ready to cook dinner for her family that evening. Now at work, the list of things she needs to accomplish seems endless. Just thinking about the day ahead makes her exhausted. She can't imagine how she will accomplish everything that needs to be done before the end of the day, much less by the weekend.

Lately Janet's been plagued by physical problems. Her exhausted body cries out through headaches, backaches, shoulder and neck tension, not to mention sheer depletion. Her family has noticed that she's not taking care of herself and has encouraged her to get some rest and relaxation. That sounds like good advice, but Janet feels there's simply not time to take care of her physical needs in her hectic schedule.

Whew! I can relate to Janet. How about you? Read over the following list of physical symptoms brought on by a stretched-to-the-max lifestyle.

stomach cramps
headaches
shortness of breath
fatigue
neck pain
racing pulse
muscle twitches
blurred vision
shakiness
unexplained rashes
jaw pain

Can you throw in some others? Truth is, the aches and pains you experience are tailored for the weak spots in your body. Stress will find its way to the vulnerable places in your particular physical makeup and then settle in for the long haul, producing pain and debilitation if you don't do something about it!

My friend, your body belongs to God, but he has housed you in it while on this earth. If it is going to be taken care of while you're here, you'll be the one to do it! It's your choice to honor God with what he has given you, and part of what he has given you is a physical body that needs proper rest, proper exercise, and proper nutrition. "Do you not know that your body is a sanctuary of the Holy Spirit who is in you, whom you have from God? You are not your own, for you were bought at a price; therefore glorify God in your body" (1 Cor. 6:19–20).

When I really grasp the reality that my body is God's temple, then it becomes my personal goal to take care of this temple—for him. I love God. I love his Holy Spirit. I can honor him and show him my love by taking care of my body, his earthly home.

When I go through periods of not getting enough sleep, exercise, or the right kinds of food, then I am dishonoring God by not taking care of his earthly home. That reality grieves me because I so long to honor him in everything I do and with everything he has given me.

Perhaps if we could always view *taking care of ourselves* as doing something for the Lord, then we would be more inclined to do so. It's just so easy, however, to get caught up in the dailiness of life and use all of our energy addressing the more pressing needs of family and work. *Too much to do* often steals our goals of taking care of our body, mind, and emotions.

That happened to Libby. It was all she could do to keep up with the demands at work and manage her household. Because of her busy lifestyle, she viewed an exercise program as a luxury. She hardly had enough energy to fix an evening meal, let alone exercise after a hard day at work. Already she was missing sleep by staying up late, taking care of things around the house.

During lunch break she usually grabbed fast food while she was running errands. Sometimes she stopped at these same fast-food restaurants after work to buy supper for her family. She often resented that some women seemed to have time to exercise regularly and fix nutritious meals at night. She decided those women just weren't as busy as she was! Libby felt that she didn't have time to eat right, exercise, and get enough rest.

Many women feel like they just don't have time to take care of themselves! In the Frazzled Female seminars when I ask, "What keeps you from exercising, eating properly, and getting enough rest?" the response in unison is, "I don't have enough time!"

Oh my, if you're running on that treadmill of *too much to do and not enough time to do it,* then it seems almost impossible to get off. You simply must make the choice and follow through with it, to take care of your physical needs!

After years of excruciating pain in my jaws and neck, brought on by a hectic lifestyle that took precedence over taking care of myself physically, I can speak from personal experience. I ended up having two surgeries with months of recovery before I learned to slow down and take better care of my body! If you don't take care of your physical needs by choice, then you will eventually be forced to deal (not by choice) with a body that succumbs to the daily stress and strain which you're placing on it.

Eating Sleeping Exercising Relaxing

Ignoring any one of these areas can make you tense, irritable, and unable to tackle even little things. Plus, the longer these areas go unattended, the more your body, your emotions, and your mind will suffer.

"Glorify God in your body" (1 Cor. 6:20). That's not a suggestion but a command straight from Scripture to take care of your physical house. And I don't see the phrase, "when you have time," dangling on the end of that command.

Now for the good part. Feel encouraged! We'll work through this together in the pages ahead.

Women who exercise regularly, eat nutritiously, and get enough sleep are better equipped to deal with stress on a daily basis. I know you're a proactive woman, one who is interested in climbing ABOVE the frazzledness of your life. Making it this far in this book is evidence of that!

I pray that you will explore ways to get better at taking care of *you* and that you'll set some goals, asking your Father to show you ways you can honor him with your body.

- ☞ In which areas do you need to better care for yourself physically?

- ☞ Eating Sleeping Exercising Relaxing

Chapter Twenty

Seeking God's Guidance

"Make Your ways known to me, LORD; teach me Your paths.
Guide me in Your truth and teach me, for You are the God
of my salvation; I wait for You all day long."
PSALM 25:4–5

Diane is exasperated. It is early evening, and she has just gotten home from work. Much of what she wanted to accomplish during her day at the office is still undone. She is tired, and her body is beginning to ache. Recently Diane's doctor told her that her physical discomfort and emotional depletion were direct results of stress. He encouraged her to find a hobby and get regular exercise—anything to keep her mind off work when she wasn't there. He gave her a pamphlet about the benefits of a regular exercise program and suggested she get started right away. "It will take a time commitment and may even interrupt your schedule, but the benefits you will experience will be well worth the inconvenience," he said. Then came the sobering words, "If you don't start taking care of yourself now, you'll pay for it later."

Sometimes we just don't consider the amount of stress we heap on our bodies. We must understand that stress has physical consequences. For example, if I allow stress to keep me from eating right, I may run out of steam and lose concentration. It's important that I accept responsibility for the choices I make. I do have control over my eating patterns. When I take ownership and realize that getting the proper nutrients can affect the way I feel, look, and behave, then I'm more motivated to eat properly.

Perhaps you are beginning to realize that something must be done to ward off physical and emotional problems that are likely headed your way because you are not taking care of your physical needs. Many times, when faced with the gloom of reality, we shift to panic mode. I encourage you to *know* that your God is not confused or even ruffled in the least about your schedule, your time limitations, and the fact that you need to devote time to taking care of yourself. He understands this and has the solution all planned out for you. His promise offers you hope that he is in control of your schedule *and your body.*

"'For I know the plans I have for you'—this is the LORD's declaration—'plans for your welfare, not for disaster, to give you a future and a hope'" (Jer. 29:11). And furthermore, he longs for you to come to him and talk with him about all your concerns. He promises to listen to you, and he wants to help you with your goals of self-improvement. "You will call to Me and come and pray to Me, and I will listen to you. You will seek Me and find Me when you search for Me with all your heart" (Jer. 29:12–13).

Carole Lewis, best-selling author of the First Place weight-loss program, puts it this way:

> It has been said that our perception of reality is our reality. If we think we are in a fog, we are in a fog. I'm glad that my God is never in a fog. Even when the darkness of my present circumstances prevents me from seeing clearly, my darkness is not dark to God. God knows where we are this very minute. He knows where we're sitting, what we're thinking and what we might be eating; and He

knows how we feel. Jesus said in Luke 12:7, "Indeed, the very hairs of your head are all numbered." Yes, God knows where we are.[3]

My dear friend, be encouraged and full of hope. God does know, he does care, and he will help you begin a lifestyle to honor your body, his temple!

Through your relationship with Jesus Christ, you can set manageable goals and make them a priority. Through prayer and Bible study, the Holy Spirit will lead you to set the goals God designs for you. He will also help you stick to them. "I am able to do all things through Him who strengthens me" (Phil. 4:13).

OK, are you ready to take some steps to begin a lifestyle that takes care of *you*?

I'm including a "work area" at the end of this chapter because I know how important it is to write down your goals. It helps you take ownership and steers you toward a positive commitment.

Spend some time thinking about where you need to improve. Perhaps you're good at taking a few rest breaks throughout the day, but you need to incorporate some exercise into your daily schedule. I know other women who take great pains to work in the exercise but quickly succumb to fast food because it's convenient to grab.

You will notice the greatest benefits from paying attention to each area. And *success* in one area can transfer to *success* in another! For instance, when I eat vegetables full of vitamins and minerals, I *feel* more like exercising than when I fill up on a meal of convenient fast food.

Please make it a point to get your Father's take on your goals. He loves you and wants you to succeed at managing your physical needs. One of my favorite verses in all the Bible is one I have committed to memory from Jeremiah. It fills me with such wonder, hope, and excitement to know that God wants me to ask him so that he can tell me!

"Call to Me and I will answer you and tell you great and wondrous things you do not know" (Jer. 33:3).

My Goals for This Week

Exercise

1. _____

2. _____

Diet/Nutrition

1. _____

2. _____

Sleep/Rest

1. _____

2. _____

Sample goals:

☞ Exercise: I will walk briskly for twenty minutes five days.

☞ Diet/nutrition: I will snack on fruit instead of crackers or candy.

☞ Sleep/rest: I will take ten minutes each afternoon to breathe deeply and refresh my mind.

Chapter Twenty-One

The Stress of Sin

"How happy is the one
whose transgression is forgiven,
whose sin is covered!
How happy is the man
the Lord does not charge with sin,
and in whose spirit is no deceit!
When I kept silent, my bones became brittle
from my groaning all day long.
For day and night Your hand was heavy on me;
my strength was drained
as in the summer's heat.
Then I acknowledged my sin to You
and did not conceal my iniquity.
I said, 'I will confess my transgressions to the Lord,'
and You took away the guilt of my sin."

PSALM 32:1–5

In the previous chapters we explored why we feel frazzled and how the effects of stress pile up when we don't take care of ourselves physically. There's another kind of stress that can place great strain on us physically, mentally, and emotionally. Often it's even more painful and debilitating. And it's the stress of unconfessed sin!

Donna often recalls the unrest she experienced several years ago. She remembers the day she went to her doctor because of shortness of breath, heart palpitations, and other physical discomforts. After an examination her doctor asked, "Are you under some kind of stress?" Actually Donna was suffering from the weight of unconfessed sin in her life. She didn't admit it at the time, but she now realizes that being out of harmony with God affected her emotionally, mentally, and physically.

Just as not attending to your physical needs can contribute to unwanted stress in your life, a complacent attitude toward sinful behavior can also lead to stress overload. Consider these damaging effects of unconfessed sins:

sleeplessness

loss of appetite

loss of joy

withdrawal from people

lack of energy

racing pulse

physical aches

inability to focus

restlessness

lack of interest

moodiness

This is just a sampling of the physical upheaval in which we place ourselves when we allow unconfessed sin to linger. David was right on target when he cried out, "When I kept silence [before I confessed], my bones wasted away through my groaning all the day long. For day and night Your hand [of displeasure] was heavy upon me; my moisture was turned into the drought of summer" (Ps. 32:3–4 AMP).

David knew the agony of unconfessed sin. Before giving his sin to God, he experienced a spiritual drought and heaviness. God did not want David (and he doesn't want you) to settle for anything less than a full and abundant life with him. And that abundant life is contingent upon confessing our sins to our heavenly Father and then turning in repentance to his thoughts and his ways. "A thief comes only to steal and to kill and to destroy. I have come that they may have life and have it in abundance" (John 10:10).

SIN is a thief and will rob you of God's blessings. When we are involved in personal sin, God may allow us to experience great physical, emotional, and mental discomfort. Discomfort is part of the refining process, drawing our wayward hearts back to him. He is always working out his plan for our lives and is consistently leading us to the place of contentment and joy in his presence. You and I will not enter that place of abundance in him if there is willful and unconfessed sin in our lives!

Remember Donna and her doctor's visit? She did not come to terms with a particular sin area in her life until her doctor asked her, "Are you under some kind of stress?" Prior to her doctor's prodding, she had shrugged off her sin as no big deal.

Unconfessed sin *is* a big deal and creates a barrier between you and God. Since the fall in the garden of Eden as described in Genesis 3, sin has been a reality for all of God's children. To rationalize sin and deny its existence in your life is to deny the truth of Scripture. "If we say, 'We have no sin,' we are deceiving ourselves, and the truth is not in us" (1 John 1:8).

We need to acknowledge the reality of sin and the need to confess. We simply do not have to live with the burden of unconfessed sin! God has promised to forgive us and to restore our joy. "If we confess our sins, He is faithful and righteous to forgive us our sins and to cleanse us from all unrighteousness" (1 John 1:9).

Please don't misunderstand what I'm saying. Physical problems are not always indicative of unconfessed sin. Many causes lead to sickness. However, it is important to realize that physical pain and suffering are possible consequences to living a sinful lifestyle. Feelings of sadness, guilt, anger, embarrassment, shame, lethargy, sickness, and despair are often experienced as consequences of sin.

God does not desire that you stay in that place of hurt, but he will allow you to experience these ailments to bring you to repentance. You may need to repent of an attitude or a behavior or even a lifestyle that is displeasing to him. From my personal experience I can certainly attest that God will not allow me to experience his peace physically, mentally, and emotionally if I'm living out of his will.

I can also testify along with the psalmist that there is a sweet release when I bring my sin before the Lord, admitting it and asking for his forgiveness. As I read David's words, I can identify with the physical breaking of chains! A weight is lifted, and a burden is dropped when we come clean before our Lord. "Then I acknowledged my sin to You and did not conceal my iniquity. I said, 'I will confess my transgressions to the LORD,' and You took away the guilt of my sin" (Ps. 32:5).

Perhaps as you read these words, you are being nudged to acknowledge and confess a sin area in your life that is displeasing to God. Often the most difficult step is taking ownership of the sin. Many times we spend countless time and energy trying to rationalize and justify our sinful behavior while the choice that would bring us abundant life is the choice of acknowledging the sin, confessing it, and then turning in repentance to get on with living!

When I consider that the negative effects of sin might be the cause of my mental, emotional, and physical discomfort, I pray the prayer of the psalmist. Then if God reveals an area of displeasure to him, I acknowledge it, confess it, and repent of it—accepting his grace and forgiveness so that I may move forward in the direction he chooses.

"Search me, God, and know my heart; test me and know my concerns. See if there is any offensive way in me; lead me in the everlasting way" (Ps. 139:23–24).

☞ Do you think you could possibly be experiencing physical, emotional, or mental distress as a result of sin?

☞ Are you willing for God to search your heart and reveal to you any areas that are creating a barrier in your relationship with him?

☞ Do you long for the sweet release that comes from acknowledging and confessing your sin?

Chapter Twenty-Two

My Identity

"I will praise the LORD at all times;
His praise will always be on my lips.
I will boast in the LORD;
the humble will hear and be glad.
Proclaim with me the LORD's greatness;
let us exalt His name together.
I sought the LORD, and He answered me
and delivered me from all my fears.
Those who look to Him are radiant with joy;
their faces will never be ashamed."

PSALM 34:1–5

Bonnie was in the middle of the wellness seminar her supervisor had asked her to attend. She had looked forward to taking a break from phones, computers, and clients, and she did enjoy learning stress tips and strategies on how to begin an exercise program. Then the instructor asked the participants to do something that was a little difficult for Bonnie. "Write a brief paragraph describing who you are." The more Bonnie considered this assignment, the more confused she felt. She could describe what she looked like and tell who she was at work. She could describe her roles of being a woman, but none of those descriptions explained *who* she was. Perplexed and a bit disturbed, she began to ponder more deeply the question, *Who am I?*

Women often tell me they share this same confusion of figuring out their identities. When we get caught up in so many roles that take us all over the place (in mind and body) on any given day, it causes us to step back and wonder, *Well, who am I anyway?* And we often want to know, *When do I stop being this person and turn into another one?*

Whoa! Life's like that. It can throw you some real zingers along the way, causing you to flounder around in confusion when God would have you realize that your true identity is in him! Colossians 3:3 says, "For you have died, and your life is hidden with the Messiah in God."

This means that if Jesus Christ lives within you, then your earthly identity is not who you really are. That earthly person, so to speak, has died, and the "real you" is nestled inside of Jesus and filled with his glory. It's hard to understand, and it's difficult to describe, but it's reality! By faith I choose to believe each day—and sometimes many times during the day—that my real life has nothing to do with what I do or who I am on this earth but everything to do with my position in Christ!

When life gets particularly stressful, I lose sight of that identity in him. Notice I did not say I *lose my identity* but that I *lose sight of it.* Especially when I mess up in a certain area or feel inadequate to do something, it's so easy for me to define my self-worth within the context of that area. Know what I mean?

This identity battle originates in the mind, and we must fight to remember that our identity is in Jesus Christ, not in who we are or what we do. When people and circumstances get us down, it's important to fight hard to remember our true identity! Joyce Meyer, best-selling author and conference host, states:

I had a wandering mind and had to train it by
discipline. It was not easy, and sometimes I still have
a relapse. While trying to complete some project,
I will suddenly realize that my mind has just wan-
dered off onto something else that has nothing to do
with the issue at hand. I have not yet arrived at a
place of perfect concentration, but at least I understand how important it is not to allow my mind to
go wherever it wishes, whenever it desires.[4]

When *my* mind wanders off, it's often in the realm of
my identity, forgetting who I am in Christ and forgetting
his power and authority to deal with each situation I face.
I'm little by little training myself to remember *whose I am*
and *who I am*. This discipline of remembrance helps keep me
focused in him as I go about my daily duties.

Another way that helps me remember my true identity
is to picture myself in my holy attire! Read the description
and visualize how you look dressed in God's righteousness.
"I greatly rejoice in the LORD, I exult in my God; for He has
clothed me with the garments of salvation and wrapped me in
a robe of righteousness, as a bridegroom wears a turban and
as a bride adorns herself with her jewels" (Isa. 61:10).

And according to King David, our glorious Father
has placed a crown upon our heads! "For You meet him with
rich blessings; You place a crown of pure gold on his head"
(Ps. 21:3).

Dear sister in Christ, I challenge you. I plead with you to
visualize yourself in your garments of salvation. This visual
image will energize you and cause you to carry yourself boldly
and regally in the midst of any trying circumstance! You may
be a wife, a mom, a coworker, a volunteer, a referee, a nurse,
an arbitrator, a counselor, the one in charge on the home
front, but first and foremost you are a daughter of the King;
and that reality, if you let it sink into your heart and soul, will
greatly impact the moments of your days.

It's a fun challenge for me to visualize myself in my holy attire when I walk into the grocery store. Believe me, I walk in with a smile on my face and a spring in my step just thinking about my robe and crown! Believe it or not, it even makes grocery shopping more pleasant. And if you ask your heavenly Father to help you remember your royalty, he will.

Months ago I was on the road, leaving one Frazzled Female event and heading to another. I was tired, a little disturbed over a recent personal situation, and feeling pretty low down on the "having it all together" scale. When I checked into the next hotel, the young man behind the desk said, "You are in the best room we have. In fact you're in the bridal suite. Someone must really think a lot of you."

My heart jumped, and I was overwhelmed with joy as the reality of *who I am* flooded throughout my body and soul. *Yes! I'm his bride, and he thinks a lot of me. In fact he loves me with an everlasting love and has reserved the best room (the bridal suite) in the house for me!*

Come on dear sister, use the creative mind God gave you and enter into the reality of who you are in Jesus. Then let that reality get all over you and splash out from your insides. Others will notice and wonder what's up with all that joy they see.

And then. Tell them!

"I delight greatly in the LORD; my soul rejoices in my God. For he has clothed me with garments of salvation and arrayed me in a robe of righteousness" (Isa. 61:10 NIV).

- ☞ Have you ever wondered who you really are?

- ☞ Perhaps now you'd like to visualize yourself dressed in your holy attire.

PART SIX

Near to the Heart of God

"Humble yourselves therefore under the mighty hand of God, so that He may exalt you in due time, casting all your care upon Him, because He cares about you."

1 PETER 5:6–7

God is always close to me whether I feel like he is or not. I make a daily choice to recognize that fact and be persistent in staying close to him!

I once heard someone say, "God is to you who you perceive him to be." That comment got me to thinking about being more creative with my picture of God. I have the type of personality that gets bored easily. So lots of times I change the way I do something just to keep from getting in a rut. Sometimes I drive a different way to work or eat dessert first. I part my hair on the other side and change the furniture around.

I've discovered that keeping spontaneous in my approach to worshipping Jesus helps me draw closer to him. There are lots of ways to be with him, maybe ways you've never thought about. Sometimes I go for a walk with him. I might sing to him or write a letter to him. Occasionally when my husband has to work late, I have dinner with him, talking with him as I eat and mulling over Scripture as I chomp on salad.

Now before you settle in on the notion that I'm totally WEIRD, why don't you explore the idea of being creative in your relationship with Jesus. Take a look at what Gary Thomas says in his book *Sacred Pathways* when he talks about people getting stuck in a rut in their relationships with God:

> Their love for God has not dimmed, they've just fallen into a soul-numbing rut. Their devotions seem like nothing more than shadows of what they've been doing for years. They've been involved in the same ministry for so long they could practically do it in their sleep. It seems as if nobody in their small groups has had an original thought for three years. They finally wake up one morning and ask, "Is this really all there is to knowing God?"[5]

Just as in my earthly relationships, growing my love for the Lord is enhanced when I try new things and change the ways I approach him. After all, life's tough, and growing your love relationship with Jesus is the most powerful antidote available to the trials of life! It's worth taking the time to explore new ways to discover his freshness and his nearness.

In this last part of the book, we are going to explore ways to keep going when your faith runs low and what to do if you experience deep depression. And we'll finish up with the wonderful reality that Jesus is praying for you right this very minute!

I'm so excited for you and want to spur you on in your faith walk, knowing that if you desire him with all your heart, soul, mind, and strength, you *will* find him!

"But from there, you will search for the LORD your God, and you will find Him when you seek Him with all your heart and all your soul" (Deut. 4:29).

Chapter Twenty-Three

The Faith Test

"May you be strengthened with all power, according to His glorious might, for all endurance and patience."

COLOSSIANS 1:11

I've had circumstances in my life when my feelings were so intertwined around people and events that it just seemed I could not muster up enough faith to see me through to the other side. Then guilt sat on top of those other feelings, compounding the intensity and making me feel helpless and hopeless!

Have you ever felt you couldn't pass the faith test? You've prayed, read your Bible, maybe even fasted, yet still you lack faith!

Let me share some hopeful (and redeeming) news with you. What you're experiencing may have nothing to do with faith at all but everything to do with feelings! We're going to take a look at the reality of faith and how our feelings can distract us and divert our attention from Jesus. That's what happened to Peter!

Immediately He made the disciples get into the boat and go ahead of Him to the other side, while He dismissed the crowds. After dismissing the crowds, He went up on the mountain by Himself to pray. When evening came, He was there alone. But the boat was already over a mile from land, battered by the waves, because the wind was against them. Around three in the morning, He came toward them walking on the sea. When the disciples saw Him walking on the sea, they were terrified. "It's a ghost!" they said, and cried out in fear.

Immediately Jesus spoke to them. "Have courage! It is I. Don't be afraid."

"Lord, if it's You," Peter answered Him, "command me to come to You on the water."

"Come!" He said.

And climbing out of the boat, Peter started walking on the water and came toward Jesus. But when he saw the strength of the wind, he was afraid. And beginning to sink he cried out, "Lord, save me!"

Immediately Jesus reached out His hand, caught hold of him, and said to him, "You of little faith, why did you doubt?" When they got into the boat, the wind ceased. Then those in the boat worshiped Him and said, "Truly You are the Son of God!" (Matt. 14:22–33)

Often there may be confusion during the storm! Peter had walked with Jesus long enough to experience his love, tenderness, and mighty power. He had listened intently to the parables about the farmer sowing his seeds, the mustard seed, and the net full of fish. He had seen Jesus miraculously feeding the five thousand people who had followed him. Peter experienced many miracles in the presence of Jesus, and the Master gave him authority to drive out evil spirits and heal diseases. How then, after walking on the water in those first few steps of faith, did Peter lose sight of Jesus and begin to sink?

It makes you wonder, doesn't it? How could he so easily forget all the things he had seen Jesus do for others and for him personally!

But you know, I can identify with Peter. I have experienced many great events—and made it through them all—with the help of Jesus. He has helped me deliver babies and lead loved ones to salvation, given me unexplainable peace on many occasions, and allowed me to witness specific answers to prayers, and yet, in spite of all those victorious moments, at other times I've focused on the storm instead of keeping my focus squarely on him!

Did I lose my faith at these times I forgot about the power of Jesus? No, I don't think so.

Romans 12:3 tells us that "God has distributed a measure of faith to each one." If you are a child of God, it is in your spiritual nature to have faith. At times, however, you might confuse your feelings with your faith. Satan uses doubt and unbelief to make you think you have to work hard to have faith. And when you just can't seem to work hard enough, he tells you your faith is lacking. The problem is not your lack of faith; it's Satan seeking to destroy your faith with lies.

For example, God provided Amy with a new job. He gave her the desire, the faith, and the ability to do her work well. She knew when she accepted the job that it was a gift from God. After a while, however, things started happening that made it difficult to enjoy her work the way she did at first. So Amy started to doubt and question herself, wondering if she really had heard from God in the first place. Was this really the job he wanted for her?

I sincerely believe that God places dreams and visions within our hearts. When he gives you a particular calling, he will also give you the desire, faith, and ability to carry through. He may call you to start a new job, teach a Bible study, or begin a family. When you receive by faith God's call on your life, he wants you to know that he has your best interest at heart. He provides for your every need in that call. It may be trusting him with the life of your child or trusting him with your finances. He loves you and wants the best for you.

There may be times, however, when the journey gets rough, that we wonder if we really heard God in the first place. That's when we must rely on our faith, instead of our feelings, to seek the truth.

In chapter 6 you read about Abraham and his journey of faith. God made him a promise, and many years later he still had not seen the results. However, Abraham *stood in faith*. He must have been attacked by doubts and unbelief, but according to Scripture he stood steadfast and unmovable. "He did not waver in unbelief at God's promise, but was strengthened in his faith and gave glory to God" (Rom. 4:20).

During this time of waiting and watching and hoping that God's promise would come to pass, Abraham kept giving glory to God! And as he did, he grew stronger and became empowered. Perhaps, unlike Peter, who placed his mind on the storm at hand instead of focusing on the Master, Abraham just praised God and thanked him for who he was.

It's a moment-by-moment choice to know that we know that our God is in control. Storms, doubts, and confusion can intimidate you. In times of trial, feelings are unpredictable and unreliable. But choosing to have faith in God has little to do with how you feel. Remember that! Don't allow feelings of worry, doubt, and confusion to keep you from experiencing the peace God wants you to enjoy as you rest in his presence.

Persevere. Keep with him. He will lead you in the way he wants you to go.

"Let me experience Your faithful love in the morning, for I trust in You. Reveal to me the way I should go, because I long for You" (Ps. 143:8).

- Is there an experience in your life where your feelings are interfering with your faith?

- Are you willing to keep praising God, giving him glory as you wait it out?

Chapter Twenty-Four

More Than a Case of the Blues

"But thanks be to God, who gives us the victory through our Lord Jesus Christ!"
1 CORINTHIANS 15:57

Have you ever been unable to shake the blues? You keep trying and trying, but you can't quite seem to feel better?

If I could beat on the drums and sound the trumpet right now, I would! Because I have good news for you, dear friend! Your body and mind may be fragile, but the Holy Spirit who lives within you is not!

I have such a heart for this topic of depression. Before experiencing it myself, I had no understanding of the debilitating effects of this illness. Being a committed Christian with a close relationship with the Lord, I felt I could pray my way out of anything. As pressures stacked up in my life, I disciplined myself to increase my prayer time.

But as weeks turned into months, my physical, emotional, and mental condition spiraled downward. I felt guilty and helpless as I desperately tried to get a grip on my life. It never occurred to me that I was getting firsthand experience on how to deal with and later teach about clinical depression.

When I finally broke down (literally) and went to my doctor for help, he asked me about stress issues in my life. He wanted to know what kind of pressures I had been dealing with and how long I had dealt with them. As I described the nature of my stress and the symptoms I was experiencing, I realized I was pretty bad off. I had never admitted the severity of my problem and certainly had never shared it with anyone else. I was Miz Superwoman Magnificat!

I, to this day, am grateful for my doctor's words: "You should not feel guilty." Hearing him say that helped me begin to release the feelings of guilt I had been heaping upon myself. The weight of guilt I was experiencing was from falling apart when I was teaching everybody else how to stay together! Now there's a smile that tickles my lips as I write about that time in my life. I was teaching stress management seminars and offering instruction on how to keep stress from becoming the unmanageable monster that it can often become. Oh yes, I knew all about how to deal with stress!

Then adding to that guilt was the guilt I experienced because of my love for the dear Lord. I remember thinking that I must not really be as close to him as I thought. I also reasoned there was some fault in my spiritual character because I could not pray my way out of this situation. To say that I felt like I was at the bottom of a black hole with an elephant sitting on my chest is not exaggerating!

To hear and then to accept the fact that I *should not feel guilty* was truly the beginning of my healing process. I later learned that many Christians who suffer from clinical depression experience this kind of guilt.

Paul speaks of how our earthly body makes us groan and long for our heavenly one: "For we know that if our earthly house, a tent, is destroyed, we have a building from God, a house not made with hands, eternal in the heavens. And, in fact, we groan in this one, longing to put on our house from heaven" (2 Cor. 5:1–2).

Amen to that! There are many times I anticipate my new body with my Lord in heaven. And I'm so thrilled that *that body* is my permanent dwelling place, not this one!

Have you, dear sister, ever felt the burden of your body, mind, and emotions? Have you longed for your permanent dwelling place in heaven where the demands of this life will be no longer occupying your every thought and movement?

Rest assured. You are already provided for! "And the One who prepared us for this very thing is God, who gave us the Spirit as a down payment" (2 Cor. 5:5).

One day you'll make your residence with God in heaven. Meanwhile, you are living in a physical body that is designed for life here on earth. Your body contains blood vessels, muscles, tissues, organs, ligaments, and various operating systems. Intricately and delicately designed, your body is your earthly tent and is susceptible to earthly wear and tear. The body doesn't work one way for Christians and another way for non-Christians. Loving the Lord does not guarantee you will be immune to the attack of stress on your body, mind, and emotions.

If you have not experienced a time of depression in your life, chances are you or someone close to you will. Developing a spiritual viewpoint on this sickness will help you respond in a biblical way. (See chapter 25 for more on depression.)

The following Scripture offered much hope and strength to me during my dark days. "The LORD is near the broken-hearted; He saves those crushed in spirit" (Ps. 34:18).

When I let go of my guilt and stopped trying to work my way out of my dark moods, I began to rest in the reality of his closeness. I began to sense his presence in the midst of my brokenness. I accepted that he was close to me and wanting to save my crushed spirit. What a comfort I began to experience!

- ☞ Are you experiencing a mood that is more than a case of the blues?

- ☞ Have you ever considered seeing a doctor about this problem?

Chapter Twenty-Five

Help Is Available

"But those who trust in the LORD will renew their strength;
they will soar on wings like eagles; they will run and
not grow weary; they will walk and not faint."

ISAIAH 40:31

Diana was trying to believe what she was reading in her morning devotional. Phrases from Isaiah kept staring back at her from her Bible: *soar on wings like eagles, run and not grow weary, walk and not faint.* It had been some time since she had gotten excited about the promises of Scripture. In fact, she seemed never to have any excitement or joy about anything these days. Things that used to bring her happiness and fulfillment, like going places with her family, now only made her feel tired and bogged down. Everything was an effort, and nothing seemed to bring her pleasure the way it once did. As Diana read Isaiah's verses again, she couldn't help wondering, *If God gives strength to the weary, why do I feel so tired and so rotten about life?*

Friend, if you have been in the throes of depression, then you understand exactly how Diana feels. Being in that place is intensified with lack of acceptance or understanding about the whole clinical depression ride. It's turbulent to say the least, causing upheaval to your psyche as well as your physical body.

Not understanding what's happening with your body, your mind, or your emotions can be exasperating and unsettling. Just know that God knows and cares about your frustration! "The LORD is the everlasting God, the Creator of the ends of the earth. He will not grow tired or weary, and his understanding no one can fathom. He gives strength to the weary and increases the power of the weak" (Isa. 40:28–29 NIV).

One way he increases the power of the weak is by increasing their understanding. If I understand more about how my body functions, then I can begin to believe that the God who controls all the parts of my body is also in control of every frustration I have concerning my body.

The brain is housed in one of the most intricate systems in the body—the central nervous system. Just as the parts of a machine are subject to wear and tear, our body systems are also prone to breakdown. In my bout with clinical depression, my brain became the faulty part.

My doctor simply explained it to me this way. "When you go through a stressful situation for a long period of time, the chemicals in your brain may begin to alter. When that happens, the chemicals that were once balanced become unbalanced, and you could enter into a period of instability, causing you mental and emotional anguish."

Strength for the Journey is a wonderfully and strategically written Bible study for those wanting to get a biblical perspective on discouragement and depression. "Nearly all people face discouragement at some time. Discouragement lasts for several days, but most individuals gradually begin to feel more positive about themselves and their circumstances. Clinical depression, on the other hand, is a state of prolonged sadness and despair."[6]

According to Dr. James Porowski and Dr. Paul Carlisle, who adapted a list from the American Psychiatric Association, to be considered depressed, a person would experience five or more of the following symptoms almost every day for a period of two weeks.

1. Depressed mood most of each day.
2. Loss of pleasure in formally enjoyable activities.
3. Significant changes in weight or appetite.
4. Can't fall asleep at night or wakes up repeatedly throughout the night.
5. Fatigue or loss of energy.
6. Feelings of hopelessness.
7. Inability to concentrate or make decisions.
8. Recurrent thoughts of death or suicide.[7]

Dear sister, this chapter was not written so I could give you medical advice. I am not equipped to offer treatment plans or to tell you what should be done if you or a loved one is experiencing depression. But I can offer you insight into this sickness by looking at its common symptoms like the ones listed above, which were the ones I experienced. If you are having these symptoms and have experienced them for a prolonged time, I lovingly encourage you to seek medical attention.

My treatment plan included medication and Christian counseling. I cannot tell you how grateful I am to have finally recognized what was going on in my brain so that I could get on the road to recovery. And full and complete recovery did occur. It was a gradual healing process but one that my Lord brought me through moment by moment.

"Do not fear, for I am with you; do not be afraid, for I am your God. I will strengthen you; I will help you; I will hold on to you with My righteous right hand" (Isa. 41:10).

> ☞ Are you or someone close to you experiencing the symptoms of clinical depression?

> ☞ Are you willing to seek medical attention?

Caring for Yourself

If you are experiencing depression, you must take care of yourself before healing can begin. Prayerfully consider these suggestions.

- Slow down. Don't try to do as much as you are accustomed to doing.
- Don't take on new activities.
- Delegate some of your responsibilities.
- Be kind to yourself when you can't accomplish what you normally accomplish.
- Plan additional time to relax during each day.
- Don't load your weekend with housework or other "catch-up" activities.
- Eat a well-balanced diet.
- Get enough sleep.
- Cut out some night activities.
- Refrain from making major decisions.
- Seek comfort from family and friends who love you.
- Spend quiet time with the Lord, resting in his presence, thinking about how much he loves you, being confident he will renew your strength.

Chapter Twenty-Six

Jesus Is Praying for You

"Any my God will supply all your needs according to
His riches in glory in Christ Jesus."

PHILIPPIANS 4:19

Elijah was a great prophet of God, one who had been used
mightily in the Lord's service, performing miracles and
boldly proclaiming his righteous acts. Elijah's life is the picture
of one who gave his all in service to the Lord. Then, in a
radical turn, he became depleted and worn. Being tired and
weary of life, he begged God to let him die.

"He sat down under a broom tree and prayed that he
might die. He said, 'I have had enough! LORD, take my life, for
I'm no better than my fathers.' Then he lay down and slept
under the broom tree" (1 Kings 19:4–5). The Father has used
the portrait of Elijah in 1 Kings time and again to encourage
and assure me of his presence in my circumstances. Like
Elijah, I have at times become weary of the circumstances of
life. And there have been times when I, just like Elijah, being
haggard and worn, have retreated to the resting place!

And you know, it's often been in that resting place, that
quiet place with the Lord that I have heard his whisper! His
whisper is unmistakable, loving, and strong!

Then He said, "Go out and stand on the mountain in the LORD's presence."

At that moment, the LORD passed by. A great and mighty wind was tearing at the mountains and was shattering cliffs before the LORD, but the LORD was not in the wind. After the wind there was an earthquake, but the LORD was not in the earthquake. After the earthquake there was a fire, but the LORD was not in the fire. And after the fire there was a voice, a soft whisper. (1 Kings 19:11–12)

This passage speaks directly to my heart's need to hear from God. Many times when I pour out my longing to him, he gives me his presence instead of my desire of the moment. And many times my desire of the moment is likened to the rushing power and turbulence of the wind, the fire, and the earthquake. It's not that our Lord doesn't reveal himself in these boisterous happenings of life. He does! But I'm finding that many times he calls me to quiet my soul and my racing heart so that he may speak to me in his whisper, full of power and grace and peace for the moment.

I remember as a teenager going through a particular event that caused me much anxiety and lots of tears. On one particular evening while I was tucked away in my bedroom crying, my older brother, Reg, came to me and offered these comforting words. "Did you know that Jesus is crying right now with you? He is crying because you are so hurt and upset." To think that Jesus really understood me and, beyond that, cared how I was feeling just touched my heart in a way that has stayed with me through all these years into my adult life.

Think of the most wonderful gift you've ever received and remember the joy and gratefulness you felt upon receiving it. Then multiply that feeling infinitely, and you'll catch a glimpse—but only a glimpse—of how Jesus feels about you.

Years after that experience in my bedroom, I learned that not only does Jesus care that much about me, but he also prays for me. Now that reality nearly blew me away, and to tell you the truth it still does!

> I pray for them. I am not praying for the world
> but for those You have given Me, because they are
> Yours. All My things are Yours, and Yours are Mine,
> and I have been glorified in them. . . . Now I am
> coming to You, and I speak these things in the
> world so that they may have My joy completed in
> them. . . . I am not praying that You take them out
> of the world but that You protect them from the evil
> one. They are not of the world, as I am not of the
> world. Sanctify them by the truth; Your word is
> truth. As You sent Me into the world, I also have
> sent them into the world. I sanctify Myself for them,
> so they also may be sanctified by the truth. . . .
> Righteous Father! The world has not known You.
> However, I have known You, and these have known
> that You sent Me. I made Your name known to them
> and will make it known, so the love You have loved
> Me with may be in them and I may be in them.
> (John 17:9–10, 13, 15–19, 25–26)

My dear friend, I believe it is critical to your growing intimacy with your Lord and Savior to grasp the reality that Jesus is praying for you! Can you believe it? Yes, do! Let that divine truth get a hold on you and fill you to the depths of your being. The King of kings and Lord of lords is lifting *you* to our Father.

Sometimes as I read that passage from John, I substitute the pronouns with my name. That helps me to further experience the tender, powerful, and unconditional love of my Lord. Knowing that Jesus is praying for *me* empowers me in ways I never thought possible.

Loving Jesus, pursuing a love relationship with him, and desiring him with all my heart, soul, mind, and strength continues radically to affect my life. Personal contact with Jesus Christ changes everything!

Oh, it's my desire that in reading *The Frazzled Female* you have been encouraged and filled with hope as you explore and commit to a lifelong, growing relationship with Jesus. He is pursuing your love and praying for you in your journey! I encourage you to enjoy your relationship with him, forever exploring his magnificent ways. Please know that as you're growing, his spirit is cheering you on and reflecting his love to those around you!

"We all, with unveiled faces, are reflecting the glory of the Lord and are being transformed into the same image from glory to glory; this is from the Lord who is the Spirit" (2 Cor. 3:18).

- ☞ Have you been quiet and still enough to hear God speak to you in his whisper?

- ☞ Does knowing Jesus is praying for you change the way you think about the trials you are experiencing?

The Frazzled Female Complete

"If I live, it will be for Christ, and if I die, I will gain even more."
PHILIPPIANS 1:21 CEV

Upon finishing *The Frazzled Female* manuscript, it is time to take all my computer folders where I had worked on each part separately and now combine them into one document. Having done that, I will call this new file, THE FRAZZLED FEMALE COMPLETE.

That's the very description of *who* I am in Jesus! Living in this world, I'm still a frazzled female, even at best. But with Jesus living inside of me, empowering me, loving me, and giving me his energy and zest for living, I'm complete in him!

My heart's yearning for you as you have journeyed through these pages is that you have allowed Jesus to birth in you and then complete in you an intense desire for a deep relationship with him. I've truly prayed that you would recognize *his yearning* for that deep relationship with you in a way you've never experienced before. The longing of his heart is that you would pull aside with him so that you may experience the depth of his love for you.

The benefits for *you* in reveling in the love of Jesus are unfathomable. As you go to that quiet place, perhaps frazzled on some days, you will emerge victoriously frazzled to face life on the good days and on those that are not so good and then even on those days that seem worse than terrible.

Just this past weekend I heard a powerful illustration about growing in love with Jesus. Being a speaker for a women's retreat in the glorious mountains of North Carolina, I was taking a dinner break and visiting with the women attending the conference. A beautiful woman in Jesus sat across the table from me and shared:

> *I went to a wedding recently, and I realized a deep spiritual truth when I later reflected on the day's events. This was a day filled with lots of wonderful things with many people surrounding the bride and groom and joining in their celebration. In order to give birth to a new little life, however, it will be necessary for this young couple to pull aside from the crowd. That's true for me! It is necessary for me to pull aside from the crowd, my daily activities, and my earthy focus to experience the deep and intimate love of Jesus and to give birth to his ways in my life.*

Oh, what a beautiful and accurate analogy. Yes, dear frazzled female friend, your heavenly Father longs to help you give birth to his love, his glory, his power and peace, so that you may glorify him as you go about your daily living. But in order for you to experience the depths of his love, you must be committed to a lifestyle of pulling aside with him so that together you and Jesus will grow this gloriously intimate relationship!

Just know that as you continue to make this choice, I'm cheering you on. But more importantly, Jesus is daily pursuing you with a passionate love and praying for you to come close to his heart.

"Father, I desire those You have given Me to be with Me where I am. Then they will see My glory" (John 17:24).

Bless you, my friend, on your journey!

How to Become a Christian

God wants us to love him above anyone or anything else because loving him puts everything else in life in perspective. In God we find the hope, peace, and joy that are possible only through a personal relationship with him. Through his presence in our lives, we can truly love one another because God is love. John 3:16 says, "For God loved the world in this way: He gave His One and Only Son, so that everyone who believes in Him will not perish but have eternal life."

In order to live an abundant life, we must accept God's gift of love. "I have come that they may have life and have it in abundance" (John 10:10).

A relationship with God begins by admitting we are not perfect. We continue to fall short of God's standards. Romans 3:23 says, "For all have sinned and fall short of the glory of God."

The price for these wrong doings is separation from God. "For the wages of sin is death, but the gift of God is eternal life in Christ Jesus our Lord" (Rom. 6:23).

God's love comes to us right in the middle of our sin. "But God proves His own love for us in that while we were still sinners Christ died for us!" (Rom. 5:8).

He doesn't ask us to clean up our lives first. In fact, without his help we are incapable of living by his standards.

Forgiveness begins when we admit our sin to God. When we do, he is faithful to forgive and restore our relationship with him. "If we confess our sins, He is faithful and righteous to forgive us our sins and to cleanse us from all unrighteousness" (1 John 1:9).

Scripture confirms that this love gift and relationship with God are not just for a special few but for everyone. "For everyone who calls on the name of the Lord will be saved" (Rom. 10:13).

If you would like to receive God's gift of salvation, pray this prayer.

Dear God, I know that I am imperfect and separated from you. Please forgive me for my sin and adopt me as your child. Thank you for this gift of life through the sacrifice of your Son. I believe Jesus died for my sins. I will live my life for you. Amen.

If you prayed this prayer for the first time, share with someone! Talk to a pastor or Christian friend. And to grow in your Christian walk, continue to cultivate your love for Jesus through Scripture study and fellowship with other Christians.

Welcome to God's family!

Notes

1. Gary Chapman, *The Five Love Languages* (Chicago, Ill.: Northfield Publishing, 1992, 1995), 140.

2. Charles Stanley, *Success God's Way* (Nashville, Tenn.: Thomas Nelson Publishers, 2000), 150, 155.

3. Carole Lewis, *Back on Track* (Ventura, Calif.: Regal Books, 2003), 26.

4. Joyce Meyer, *Battlefield of the Mind* (Tulsa, Okla.: Harrison House, 1995), 88.

5. Gary L. Thomas, *Sacred Pathways* (Grand Rapids, Mich.: Zondervan, 2002), 15.

6. James P. Porowski and Paul B. Carlisle, *Strength for the Journey* (Nashville, Tenn.: LifeWay Press, 1999), 23.

7. Ibid., 24.